Henry Ierson

## Notes on the Amended English Bible

With special reference to certain texts in the revised version of the Old and New

Testaments bearing upon the principles of Unitarian Christianity

Henry Ierson

**Notes on the Amended English Bible**
*With special reference to certain texts in the revised version of the Old and New Testaments bearing upon the principles of Unitarian Christianity*

ISBN/EAN: 9783337097882

Printed in Europe, USA, Canada, Australia, Japan

Cover: Foto ©Lupo / pixelio.de

More available books at **www.hansebooks.com**

# NOTES

ON THE

# AMENDED ENGLISH BIBLE

WITH SPECIAL REFERENCE TO CERTAIN TEXTS IN THE

## REVISED VERSION

OF THE

## OLD AND NEW TESTAMENTS

BEARING UPON THE PRINCIPLES OF

## UNITARIAN CHRISTIANITY.

BY

### HENRY IERSON, M.A.

BRITISH AND FOREIGN UNITARIAN ASSOCIATION,
ESSEX HALL, ESSEX STREET, STRAND, LONDON.

1887.

# CONTENTS.

—+—

iv CONTENTS.

# PREFACE.

We have happily now an amended English Bible. One has only to remember how the Scriptures in the Authorized Version were commonly talked about not many years ago, to appreciate the importance of this fact. The strongest charge that used to be made in disparagement of those who protested against corrupt texts and incorrect translations of the Bible, was that they were tampering with the Word of God. It is now admitted that the old Version needed correcting, and that the plea urged by Unitarians for a purer Scripture was not made without solid, reasonable grounds. There is still ample room for further amendment; and when the time for it comes, as it certainly must before very long, the work already done will render it easier to make a more thorough revision upon simple critical and scholarly principles; but there is no good reason in the meanwhile for any hesitation to adopt for public use the Version now completed. It is clearly upon the whole a great improvement on the older work, so far as it goes, and the more it is studied and used, the more will it be felt to go a long way towards what is really wanted.

The intense eagerness with which the publication of the New Testament Revision was received arose, no doubt, in some degree from curiosity, and it is probable that many ordinary readers have not even yet fully realized the immense difference it makes, that they have now a new, though it be only a revised Version of the Scriptures placed in their hands. But it will be indeed unfortunate if the public are not encouraged to make good use of their present advantages. The time for finality in such matters is past. Newer light will come, and men ought to welcome it as it comes, which they will readily do if once they are enabled to perceive why the learned study these writings with so much loving interest, and that it is a nation's literature they have to deal with in the Bible, and not an anomalous collection of mysterious oracles. Many writers have shown the sterling value of numerous corrections in the Revised Version besides those bearing upon special doctrines; but what is really wanted is that the people should be trained in the scholarly habit of free and conscientious study of Scripture, as they will never be so long as the old, erroneous Version is adhered to from mere slavish routine. It will be to render an enormous service to the growth of Christendom in religious intelligence and charity if its scholars and teachers will really help the people to appreciate the wealth of improvement now for the first time laid open to all, and with commanding authority, in the Revised Version of the Bible; which is indeed, to the English-speaking people everywhere, in a really important practical sense, almost a new revelation.

In treating with necessary brevity so large a number of texts as are here quoted or referred to, the writer can hardly hope that he has always succeeded in making clear to other minds the points of remark which, with all the information before him, were very clear to his own, or that errors of reference may not possibly have escaped attention. It is also possible that other amendments may be found in the

Revised Version which might properly have been noticed, though it will probably appear that the chief crucial passages have been pointed out by opponents, especially by the two leading Quarterly reviewers. The author would wish, however, to say that he has at least aimed at doing the work thoroughly, and with all the care needed to make it useful. Undoubtedly studies of this kind, to be perfectly successful, require a concentrated devotion of undistracted time and interest, which is not at every one's command. And it was not at first intended to do more than bring together certain well-known passages in which the Revised Version had followed the lines of our older Unitarian critics and expositors. But the work has grown under the writer's hands, the number of important amended texts having been found much greater than was at first supposed. It has been also on this account that the method of exhibiting in full the old and the new forms of each passage could not be strictly adhered to ; but care has been taken to facilitate the study of the various texts by the Index at the end of the volume, in which will be found not only references to the passages cited, but also a general intimation of what they contain.

# ERRATA.

Page 24, line 19, on Ex. xxii. 28, should read, "changing 'the gods' of the Authorized Version to 'God,'" and putting ' or, *the judges*,' in the margin.

  „  39,   „   29, instead of ' 2 Tim. i. 13' read 'i. 14.'

  „  63,   „   14,      „    'John i. 2' read 'i. 3.'

# INTRODUCTION.

ALL those who value the Scriptures may congratulate themselves on the general results of the work of the British and
American scholars of various denominations to whom was
entrusted the grave and arduous duty of amending the English
Version of the Old and New Testaments. The Revised
Version of the New Testament which appeared in 1881,
and that of the Old Testament which was published in 1885,
have brought ordinary English readers nearer to the true
sense of the Biblical writers; an immense boon on many
accounts, whatever views may be held respecting the Bible
and its contents. It is of manifest importance that known
errors should not be perpetuated either in the text or the
translation of such a volume, and that the people generally
should be put in possession, so far as was possible, of the
information on these matters which has too long been the
sole property of the learned.

The Bible will not suffer in their estimation of its true
value from the better understanding of it which is thus
placed within the reach of every one; and it will be no
slight blessing, but something to be very thankful for, if the
authority of the Bible shall cease to be quoted in defence
of theological ideas which, though they appear in certain
Creeds, are in truth neither reasonable nor Scriptural. The
Scriptures, indeed, may now be searched by English readers
with the conviction that they have before them a Version not
indeed in all respects perfect, but much nearer perfection
than the old Version, and as correct as it was perhaps possible to make it under the circumstances, and they can better

B

judge for themselves as to the real force of numerous texts which have played a great part in many a grave doctrinal controversy.

It has been asserted that not one of the numerous alterations which have been made in the Authorized Version affected 'one tittle or iota of the Christian faith,' meaning by this the sum of Church dogmas. How far this is true will be seen from the following pages. We believe that much of the ground on which certain Church dogmas have been maintained has been cut away by the removal of spurious passages and interpolated phrases, and by the correction of many serious errors of translation. The reader has only to compare the old form with the new, to understand how great has been the gain to liberal theology.

Amongst the number of new versions of the Scriptures which have been published by learned men connected with the Unitarian body, two will be here specially referred to, because they were issued by Unitarian societies, and might be understood therefore to represent at least a prevailing tendency of opinion at their respective dates: (1) The Improved Version of the New Testament, which was published by the Unitarian Fund Society in 1808. It was based upon the revised translation of Archbishop Newcome, Primate of Ireland. The Version was severely criticised by some learned Unitarians of the time, and it is not now referred to as by any means a model translation; but the extreme injustice with which it was treated by the mass of Trinitarian writers will be perceived when it is seen how many of the emendations now adopted in the Revised Version were anticipated by it. (2) The Revised Translation of the Old Testament, which the British and Foreign Unitarian Association published in 1862. It was the work of three well-known Unitarian ministers, Charles Wellbeloved, John Scott Porter, and George Vance Smith, afterwards a member of the New Testament Revision

Company. When either of these authors is quoted in the following pages, it will generally be with reference to his part in this 'Revised Translation' of 1862.

It would have been easy to show, had space permitted, that with regard to most of the emendations suggested by these and other learned men of the Unitarian body, they were supported by scholars of other denominations. References of this kind have been of necessity very few. If, however, an exception was to be made, all will admit the value and force of our quotations from Dean Alford, who, though a decided orthodox Churchman, was in every sense of the word a genuine scholar, and an earnest and able Biblical commentator.

The studious reader of the Revised Version will readily discover that many of its marginal notes are of special importance. They often serve as the true key to the meaning of the text, and whoever would use the Revision properly will carefully observe the variations of the margin. These notes are given in full in these pages at the end of each quotation. If not always pertinent to the occasion for which the texts are cited, they will be found generally instructive, and they will also illustrate to some extent the difficulties which are necessarily involved in the work of translation from old books written in languages no longer living.

It must be borne in mind by the reader that the object in view in this pamphlet is chiefly to point out certain passages in the Scriptures in which the Revision offers some amendment bearing upon particular controverted doctrines. It is remarkable that so many of these changes occur in what have been considered orthodox proof-texts, the Revisers adopting corrections which have long been contended for by Unitarian scholars. In a few instances, however, the alterations tend in the opposite direction. These are not unnoticed in the following pages.  But in the main the immense advantage appears on the side of what we have considered the more trustworthy readings and the more scholarly translations.

Justifying their theological views, as the older Unitarians did, by appeal to the Scriptures reasonably interpreted, and believing, as Unitarians still believe, that the true Scripture in its essence and spirit is not out of harmony with the practical religious doctrine of Christian Unitarianism, the upholders of that doctrine naturally joined with the learned men of other bodies in urging the necessity for amending acknowledged faults in the Authorized Version.  But the interest of our study of the Bible has never been limited to the object of securing more enlightened views of disputed passages.  The improvements made in the Revised Version are of various kinds, and many of them most important, which it did not lie within the purpose of these 'Notes' to refer to.  One point, however, of some moment, not alluded to in these pages, should not be overlooked.  In their Preface the Revisers of the Old Testament state in a few words what should be the aim of every genuine translation, 'to give to modern readers a faithful representation of the meaning of the original documents.'  But, for the headings of chapters and pages which they were directed to revise they found of course no originals, and both Companies wisely agreed to pass over this instruction 'as involving questions which belong rather to the province of the commentator than to that of the translator.'  Considering the marked theological bias of the old head-lines, especially in the Psalms and the Prophets, we cannot but regard their omission as a substantial liberal gain.

It should be observed that no attempt is here made to criticise the Revision, or to go behind either its readings or its renderings.  It is dealt with simply as it will appear to the ordinary English reader.  Nor is any question raised as to whether the New Version might not be still further improved. The 'Notes' assume that the corrections in the Revised Version are such as the occasion called for, and proceed generally on the supposition that these amendments have been rightly made. Little is aimed at, therefore, beyond drawing attention to certain of the adopted or suggested changes which obviously bear upon well-known theological doctrines, and this with the more effect that the four Companies of Revisers represented in overwhelming numbers the churches in which these doctrines are held as more or less fundamental beliefs.

In the numerous controversies of past times in relation to these doctrines, it has been a common practice to treat Scriptural texts as though they were all of equal authority, without consideration of the particular circumstances under which they were written, or even of their contexts ; and texts were pitted against texts taken with little discrimination from writings of different ages, and meanings were attributed to them which in many cases could not possibly have been in the intention of the authors. It is certainly not in the spirit of these 'Notes' to follow in the track of such unhistoric treatment of texts and their interpretation. When it is made clear what are the original texts, and what they really say, the way will be opened for a fair reconsideration of their theological value. The grand point is to know in regard to Scripture what are the real facts. And if as the result of such study the Scriptures are shown to present a very different view of certain doctrines, and even for some of them to furnish no authority whatever, not only will much have been gained in point of scholarship, but light is thrown upon the true development of religious thought, and the field of doctrine itself is cleared for new and better cultivation. It is a grand thing that the Scriptures should be more intelligently read, and that the immense fresh light upon their varied teachings may now be expected to produce its natural effect upon the religious thinking of the modern time.

There are, perhaps, many persons who will question the
value of any amendments in controverted texts excepting as
matters of ecclesiastical, or possibly of historic or antiquarian
interest; and it may be regretted that the work of revising
was not taken in hand long since, when the Bible was more
implicitly and more generally believed in as the one great
ultimate authority in religion and morals than is the case in
these later times; but it is worth consideration whether
even twenty or ten years earlier the revision could have been
made as well as it has now been done. The age of textual
controversy upon the lines just indicated is undoubtedly
past, but surely not the period of reasonable, scientific study
of the Scriptures, which, indeed, is a thing quite modern.

It has not been thought necessary to quote all the passages
in every case of correction of which examples have been
given; and, besides, the limits of space had to be considered,
so that only a somewhat disjointed selection of texts could
be made. This was unavoidable, especially if the Old and
the New Versions were to be placed side by side, as seemed
almost a necessity if the reader is asked to note certain
differences between them.

But there will also be felt a sense of incompleteness and
want of proportion in the treatment of the various topics;
since though, as we have observed, the Revision gives manifest advantage to the liberal view of Scripture doctrine upon
perhaps every point of its old contention with orthodoxy, in
some cases there would naturally be only a small number of
corrections, in others more, quite independently of the weight
of subject; and it was not intended to offer a treatise on the
whole theology of these questions. That is a work which
may well be taken up anew by liberal theologians with the
aid of the now accredited revisions. In these pages may be
found some helpful material for a work of the kind, and this
is all that the writer has undertaken to furnish.

# THE SCRIPTURES, AND THE WORD OF GOD.

2 TIM. iii. 16.

| *Authorized Version.* | *Revised Version.* |
|---|---|
| All Scripture is given by inspiration of God, and is profitable for doctrine, for reproof, for correction, for instruction in righteousness, that the man of God may be perfect, throughly furnished unto all good works. | Every scripture inspired of God is also profitable for teaching, for reproof, for correction, for instruction * which is in righteousness: that the man of God may be complete, furnished completely unto every good work. |
| | [* Or, *discipline.* |

So, in substance, the Improved Version translated; 'All Scripture given by inspiration of God, is profitable,' &c., adding in a note, 'Thus it is not defined what Scripture was divinely inspired.' And according to the Revised Version also, that question is not here determined. Yet this text has been constantly quoted in defence of the inspiration and consequent infallible authority of every statement, every chapter and line, even every word, in the common Bible. The preceding context, 'that from a babe thou hast known the sacred writings which are able to make thee wise unto salvation,' shows that the writer had in his mind the practical value of certain inspired teachings, and that he was referring to them in this sense of profitableness.

It will prove a great advantage if the Revised Version shall be found to have given to the Bible-reading public a more just view than has been commonly held respecting the real character of the original Scriptures. They may no longer worship the letter of the Bible, but they will more clearly understand its spirit.

1 PET. iv. 11.

| *Authorized Version.* | *Revised Version.* |
|---|---|
| If any man speak, *let him speak* as the oracles of God; if any man minister, let him do it as of the ability which God giveth. | If any man speaketh, *speaking* as it were oracles of God; if any man ministereth, *ministering* as of the strength which God supplieth. |

The idea of a Bible which is in every page of it an oracular declaration of the mind of God, to which all orthodox Christian teaching must conform, is not favoured by the new Version. The writer is referring here to the present inspiration of the Spirit, as Dr. Macknight explains. The speaker is to utter faithfully 'what hath been revealed to him,' not to regulate what he says by reference to some old, authoritative, infallible rule.

----

A similar passage occurs in Rom. (xii. 6), in which the phrase, 'the proportion (or analogy) of faith,' has been usually understood to indicate a certain scheme of doctrines as constituting a rule or test by which any new prophesying must be guided or tried. Such an idea, as Dean Alford pointed out, the context does not support. The Revisers, with him, as also with the Improved Version, translate in the text, 'let us prophesy according to the proportion of our faith.' The Apostle is not alluding to a settled rule of faith, as Calvin and others supposed, but to his previous expression in *v.* 3, 'as God hath dealt to each man a measure of faith.'

----

A passage from the Old Testament has been often cited to prove that the Scriptures are 'the final appeal in all controversies of religion,' to use the language of the Westminster Confession of Faith, in which the words are quoted as a proof-text—

## Is. viii. 20.

*Authorized Version.*

And when they shall say unto you, Seek unto them that have familiar spirits, and unto wizards that peep and mutter : should not a people seek unto their God? for the living to the dead? To the law and to the testimony : if they speak not according to this word, it is because there is no light in them.

*Revised Version.*

And when they shall say unto you, Seek unto them that have familiar spirits, and unto the wizards that chirp and that mutter : should not a people seek unto their God? on behalf of the living *should they seek* unto the dead? To the *law and to the testimony! †if they speak not according to this word, surely there is no morning for them.

[* Or, *teaching.* † Or, *surely according to this word shall they speak for whom there is no morning.*

The passage is a difficult one, and the sense not easy to determine, but the Revisers appear to agree with Bishop Lowth that the translation, 'there is no light in them,' is clearly inadmissible. The final authority of Scripture in settlement of doctrinal controversies is manifestly not the thing present to the mind of the Prophet.

———

'Search the Scriptures,' in the discourse of Jesus, John v. 39, has been made the text of many sermons on the divine inspiration of every part of the Bible. This admirable counsel is now, however, placed in the margin, and it is represented as at least more probable that Jesus said, 'Ye search,' &c., a translation which the context seems clearly to justify.

———

## Matt. v. 21.

Ye have heard that it was said by them of old time, Thou shalt not kill.

Ye have heard that it was said to them of old time, Thou shalt not kill.

This form is repeated and the same correction is made

in *v*. 33. (In *v*. 27 the Revisers omit 'by them of old time,' as also does the Improved Version.) The correction is important because it makes the point clear that Jesus was referring to the actual written Mosaic Law, and not merely to old Hebrew usage and opinion. Did he then believe that 'God spake all these words' (Ex. xx. 1), to which he was applying so bold an interpretation and enlargement? It is usually supposed that in *v*. 33 he was referring to one of 'these words,' commonly called the third commandment. But if so, he certainly puts another of his own in place of it, viz. 'Swear not at all.' And, in *v*. 38, he distinctly reverses the law (Ex. xxi. 24) which Moses was commanded to set before the people as the law of God. He did not hold the modern doctrine that everything contained in the Bible must be regarded as of divine inspiration.

Those also who have been taught that every word of at least the original writings has been preserved as a word of God by the interposition of Divine Providence, will receive unexpected enlightenment in discovering the frequent uncertainties of the original text, as often implied, and sometimes plainly indicated, in the marginal notes and variations. They will see how difficult it is in many passages to determine what the writers really said. The following is a simple example, one out of many—

### MARK i. 2.

*Authorized Version.*

As it is written in the Prophets, Behold, I send my messenger before thy face, which shall prepare thy way before thee. The voice of one crying in the wilderness, Prepare ye the way of the Lord, make his paths straight.

*Revised Version.*

Even as it is written in Isaiah the prophet,* Behold, I send my messenger before thy face, who shall prepare thy way. The voice of one crying in the wilderness, Make ye ready the way of the Lord, make his paths straight.

[* Some ancient authorities read, *in the prophets.*

There has been obviously some mistake here ; if this was not made by the original writer in attributing to Isaiah a passage not to be found in his writings, then it must be supposed that the passage from Malachi, the first quoted, was an interpolation; or, if the original contained this, then either the transcribers in some of the manuscripts inserted the name Isaiah, or others, if it was in the original, omitted it, and, observing that there were two quotations from different authors, inserted 'prophets' instead.   There is no historical difficulty on either supposition, if these writings are dealt with in the ordinary way.   Variations of this kind are of common occurrence in all ancient writings.   But there is insuperable difficulty if the writers are believed to have been in any sense the mere organs of an oracular inspiration, and therefore above the reach of reasonable criticism.

It should be further observed that the writers of the Gospels follow the Septuagint in omitting 'in the desert' in the second clause from Isaiah.   The Revisers of the Old Testament appear to have translated more correctly the original text, if we may judge from the Hebrew parallelism, and from the general drift of the passage ; but if they are right, the quotation in the New Testament can hardly be upheld as infallibly accurate—

Is. xl. 3.

| *Authorized Version.* | *Revised Version.* |
|---|---|
| The voice of him that crieth in the wilderness, Prepare ye the way of the LORD, make straight in the desert a highway for our God. | The voice of one that crieth,* Prepare ye in the wilderness the way of the LORD, make straight† in the desert a highway for our God. |
|  | [* Or, *that crieth in the wilderness.*   † Or, *level.* |

## ORTHODOXY AND HERESY.

On the important question of salvation by the holding of certain opinions or beliefs, the observant reader will find much instructive suggestion particularly in the marginal notes of the Revised Version. For example, an expression often used by bigoted persons, 'sound in the faith,' occurs in Tit. i. 13 and ii. 2. The Revisers keep the words in the text, but they explain that 'sound' means 'healthy' or 'healthful;' and in *v.* 9 of the first chapter, 'sound doctrine' becomes in the margin 'the healthful teaching,' as also in ii. 1, and in 1 Tim. i. 10 and 2 Tim. iv. 3. The following passage fairly exhibits the variation :

2 TIM. i. 13.

| *Authorized Version.* | *Revised Version.* |
|---|---|
| Hold fast the form of sound words which thou hast heard of me. | Hold the pattern of sound* words which thou hast heard from me.    [* Gr. *healthful.* |

---

ROM. vi. 17.

| | |
|---|---|
| But ye have obeyed from the heart that form of doctrine which was delivered you. | Ye became obedient from the heart to that form* of teaching whereunto ye were delivered.<br><br>[* Or, *pattern.* |

The metaphor is said to be that of a mould into which metal is cast.

The idea of a particular scheme of doctrine necessary to be believed in order to obtain salvation cannot now be supported by this passage. So is there no longer the suggestion of an orthodoxy of belief in the following allusion to the fact that Titus had received the gospel which Paul preached, by which, therefore, both could alike be blessed, though the one was a Jew, the other a Gentile—

TIT. i. 4.

| | |
|---|---|
| To Titus, mine own Son after the common faith. | To Titus, my true child after a common faith. |

A similar expression occurs in Jude, *v.* 3, 'to write unto you of the common salvation' (in the Revised Version 'our common salvation'), in connection with which the author would urge a contending earnestly 'for the faith which was once delivered unto the saints.' (See also *v.* 20). The Revisers have given to this faith what looks like a stamp of dogmatic finality by translating 'once for all' instead of 'once,' the usual translation. Compare *v.* 5, the only other place in which the change could have been made. But the whole Epistle has rather a practical aim, and is directed against an immoral perversion, 'turning the grace of our God into lasciviousness,' and so denying Christ in reality under the very guise of his name.

---

Another passage which has been conceived to imply that a certain set of beliefs is necessary to be held in Christian profession, is to be found in the Epistle to the Hebrews. But faith is not the thing in question in the text so often cited to support the idea of a Christian orthodoxy. In the Improved Version the word is rendered, not faith, but hope.

### HEB. X. 23.

| *Authorized Version.* | *Revised Version.* |
|---|---|
| Let us hold fast the profession of our faith without wavering. | Let us hold fast the confession of our hope that it waver not. |

---

How the terms 'heresy,' 'heretical,' are used in the New Testament may be observed in the following passages :

### ACTS xxiv. 14.

| After the way which they call heresy, so worship I the God of my fathers. | After the way which they call a sect,* so serve I the God of our fathers. |
|---|---|
| | [* Or, *heresy.* |

Which is the translation of the Improved Version. The word is used several times in Acts in the same sense.

### Tit. iii. 10.

| *Authorized Version.* | *Revised Version.* |
|---|---|
| A man that is an heretic after the first and second admonition, reject. | A man that is heretical\* after a first and second admonition, refuse.† |
| | [\* Or, *factious.*     † Or, *avoid.* |

The same kind of note in 1 Cor. xi. 19 brings out the practical character of New Testament heresy, that it means something factious and tending to division, and has nothing to do with sincere differences of opinion. So also Gal. v. 20, ' The works of the flesh are . . . factions, divisions, heresies ' (marg. ' or, *parties* ').

### Jude 22.

| And of some have compassion, making a difference. | And\* on some have mercy who† are in doubt. |
|---|---|
| | [\* The Greek text in this passage (And . . . . fire) is somewhat uncertain.    † Or, *while they dispute with you.* |

That some correction was here needed the English reader will at once perceive from the absolute abandonment of the Authorized translation ; but he cannot but observe with respect the straightforward indication given in the margin, that in some passages at least of the New Testament, as has been remarked, there is great uncertainty as to the original text. He may the more readily receive the precept of tolerance which now appears in the Revised text.

## INFIDELITY AND UNBELIEF.

' Infidel' is one of the misleading terms which now drop out of the Bible. In 2 Cor. vi. 15, the Revised text reads, ' What portion hath a believer with an unbeliever ?' not 'an infidel,' as in the Authorized Version ; and in 1 Tim. v. 8, he that provides not for his family is said to deny the faith, and to be 'worse than,' not 'an infidel,' but 'an unbeliever,' the distinction in both cases being between a Christian and a non-Christian, implying no question of religious opinions at all, but one of religious profession and consistency of action therewith, while to 'deny the faith' clearly means to be living in opposition to Christian principles. It is apostasy of character, not of opinions, that is reprehended.

In the following passage the context shows that the Revised Version conveys more accurately the meaning of the original. The text simply describes the punishment of a servant who had not done his duty. There is no reference to belief or unbelief:

LUKE xii. 46.

| *Authorized Version.* | *Revised Version.* |
| --- | --- |
| And will appoint him his portion with the unbelievers. | And appoint his portion with the unfaithful. |

That saving faith, in the New Testament, is not to be identified with creeds or opinions, may be inferred from the following correction:

JOHN iii. 36.

| He that believeth on the Son hath everlasting life; and he that believeth not the Son shall not see life. | He that believeth on the Son hath eternal life; but he that obeyeth* not the Son shall not see life.   [* Or, *believeth not.* |

So in Rom. xv. 31, the Authorized 'them that do not believe, in Judea,' now reads in the Revised, with Alford's Version, 'them that are disobedient.' In Heb. xi. 31, 'them that believed not,' reads, 'them that were disobedient.' See also Rom. xi. 31. The following passage exhibits the same suggestive amendment:

HEB. iv. 11.

| That no man fall after the same example of unbelief. | That no man fall after* the same example of disobedience.   [* Or, *into,* Gr. *in.* |

'Because of your little faith,' Matt. xvii. 20, is an obvious improvement on 'because of your unbelief.' But it is a different reading, not a corrected translation.

## USE OF THE TERMS, MYSTERY, WISDOM, SCIENCE, PHILOSOPHY.

1 COR. ii. 1.

| *Authorized Version.* | *Revised Version.* |
|---|---|
| I came not with excellency of speech, or of wisdom, declaring unto you the testimony of God. | I came not with excellency of speech,* or of wisdom, proclaiming to you the mystery† of God. |
| | [* Or, *word*.   † Many ancient authorities read, *testimony*. |

'The testimony of God' is an unusual expression, but 'the mystery of God' is a phrase which occurs elsewhere.  For example, 'Then is finished the mystery of God, according to the good tidings which he declared to his servants the prophets' (Rev. x. 7, R.V.).  We find also the mystery of the kingdom of God, the mystery, or secret, hidden in God from past ages, but now made known ; the mystery of the gospel, of godliness, and of the faith.  But the New Testament use of the term 'mystery' gives no sanction to the common idea that religion involves belief in incomprehensible or contradictory propositions.  The opening of the door of salvation to the Gentile world through the death of Christ was in the present instance the revelation of that mystery of God to which Paul frequently refers.

---

1 COR. i. 20, 21.

| Hath not God made foolish the wisdom of this world? | Hath not God made foolish the wisdom of the world? |
|---|---|
| For after that, in the wisdom of God, the world by wisdom knew not God, it pleased God by the foolishness of preaching to save them that believe. | For seeing that in the wisdom of God the world through its wisdom knew not God, it was God's good pleasure through the foolishness of the* preaching to save them that believe. |
| | [* Gr. *thing preached*. |

It was not by wisdom that the world was misled, but by the particular schemes of opinion which it regarded as wisdom ; and it is with this unsound preconception the Apostle contrasts the gospel which he taught, *the* preaching which, though the world of that time failed to apprehend it in its divine truth and force, justifies itself also to the modern mind in proportion as it becomes better understood. Foolishness of any sort in preaching is the last thing he would have commended.

---

### Col. ii. 8.

| *Authorized Version.* | *Revised Version.* |
|---|---|
| Beware lest any man spoil you through Philosophy and vain deceit. | Take heed lest there shall be any one that maketh spoil of you through his philosophy and vain deceit. |

The Apostle is not to be understood as discrediting philosophy, but only the ill-grounded assumption of it which was so commonly made at the time for purposes of profit. There were those who turned the Christian profession to the same perverted use, 'supposing that godliness is a way of gain' (1 Tim. vi. 5). The Revised Version has here a great improvement on the Authorized 'supposing that gain is godliness.' The Improved Version had the same correction.

It is gratifying to find that in the Revised Version the text does not appear of which many ignorant persons have made a deplorable use, as though Christianity had been set by an inspired writer in antagonism with scientific truth. Instead of 'oppositions of science, falsely so called,' we now read, 'oppositions of the knowledge which is falsely so called' (1 Tim. vi. 20). This was probably the beginning of the fanciful 'Gnosis' that had so much to do with the genesis of the Church orthodoxy, a very different thing from the patient and sober study of facts, or science properly so called.

## THE TRINITY.

### I JOHN V. 7.

| *Authorized Version.* | *Revised Version.* |
|---|---|
| For there are three that bear record in heaven, the Father, the Word, and the Holy Ghost, and these three agree in one. | [This text is simply dropped out of the Bible, without even a marginal note, and a new 7th verse is made out of the end of v. 6 to take its place.[1]] |

'These celebrated words,' says Mr. Sharpe,[2] 'are omitted by all critical editors, because not found in any Greek manuscript that was written before the invention of printing. They are the only words in the Bible which directly support the Athanasian Trinity of Father, Word, and Holy Ghost.' The editors of the Improved Version anticipated the Revisers in omitting this verse, stating in a note the incontrovertible reasons for regarding it as spurious, added by a later hand, and not the work of the original author. But it is now decided that the passage has never really formed part of the Sacred Writings. No educated person can henceforth refer to this text as containing Scriptural doctrine in opposition to the Unitarian belief.

---

### MATT. xxviii. 19.

| | |
|---|---|
| Go ye therefore, and teach all nations, baptizing them in | Go ye therefore, and make disciples of all the nations, |

---

[1] In some other instances of verses omitted in the Revised Version no attempt has been made to disguise the omission, e.g. Matt. xvii. 21, 'This kind goeth not out but by prayer and fasting.'

[2] In a short tract, now out of print, which was compiled on the same method that is here adopted. It was entitled, 'Controversial Texts Corrected; or, a Selection of Texts from the New Testament, which either through Mistakes in the Translation, or from Faultiness in the Greek Manuscript used by the early Translators, have been made to give countenance to the Popular Doctrines of the Trinity, the proper Deity of Jesus, and the Atonement.' Mr. Sharpe's notes referred to in the present publication are mostly contained in this tract.

| *Authorized Version.* | *Revised Version.* |
|---|---|
| the name of the Father, and of the Son, and of the Holy Ghost. | baptizing them into the name of the Father, and of the Son, and of the Holy Ghost. |

' Into the name of' was the translation also of the Improved Version. The Greek preposition is the same as will be found in 1 Cor. x. 2, where of the Israelites in the wilderness it is said in the Authorized Version, they 'were all baptized unto Moses in the cloud and in the sea,' which the Revised Version leaves unaltered, but says in the margin, ' or, *into.*' In a similar case in Acts the Revisers translate 'into,' preferring this to the Authorized ' unto :' 'And he said (Acts xix. 3), Into what then were ye baptized? And they said, Into John's baptism.' Then follows verse 5, as transcribed below. That this was the formula actually used by the Apostles may be seen in corrections of the Revised Version such as the following, which were anticipated in each instance in the Improved Version. These clearly explain the few other cases where the word ' in' is employed. The second passage indicates clearly the force of the ' into,' the correct translation.

### ACTS xix. 5.

| When they heard this they were baptized in the name of the Lord Jesus. | And when they heard this they were baptized into the name of the Lord Jesus. |
|---|---|

### 1 COR. i. 13, 15.

| Was Paul crucified for you? or were ye baptized in the name of Paul? 15. Lest any should say that I had baptized in mine own name. | Was Paul crucified for you? or were ye baptized into the name of Paul? 15. Lest any man should say that ye were baptized into my name. |
|---|---|

The change in these instances appears so slight that the effect of the correction, and the decisive alteration of the sense and purport of the text produced by it, may be scarcely at first apparent. It is, however, clear that baptizing into the

name of Paul could only have meant baptizing into the profession of discipleship to Paul.   So the nations were to be
made, with the accompanying sign of baptism, disciples of
the faith indicated, in God, the One only God the Father,
in his Son Jesus Christ, and in his Holy Spirit.

The idea is the same in 2 Cor. xiii. 14, where the Apostle
desired that the brethren might be blest with the grace of the
Lord Christ, the love of God, and the communion or equal
participation and enjoyment of his Holy Spirit.   All this is
extremely unlike the kind of thought suggested in the Authorized Version of Christ's last injunction to his disciples.   The
phrase is commonly used as a kind of adjuration ; churches
are dedicated, and associations of various kinds consecrated,
' in the name of the Father and of the Son and of the Holy
Ghost,' with mystic reference to a Triune God.   The Revisers
do not alter the term 'Holy Ghost' in the text last mentioned, but they insert the note, ' or, Holy Spirit.'

These are the three chief proof-texts in the Confession of
the Westminster Assembly in support of the doctrine of the
Trinity.   The first is gone.   It is acknowledged to have
never been really a part of the Bible.   The second has un-
dergone a marked change in its evident purport.   The third
relates to what Unitarians in common with other Christians
believe ; the love of God, his gift of pitying and helpful grace
in Christ, and the spiritual power of his inspiring presence
in the souls of earnest and faithful men, as we read in Heb.
vi. 4 : ' who were once enlightened, and tasted of the heavenly gift, and were made partakers of the Holy Ghost' (' or,
Holy Spirit,' see note, Heb. ii. 4).   The three ideas are
brought together in another very practical form in Jude 20 :
' Praying in the Holy Spirit, keep yourselves in the love of
God, looking for the mercy of our Lord Jesus Christ unto
eternal life,' where the previous reference to evil persons
' having not the Spirit' explains the preference of the Revisers
for the term Spirit instead of the Authorized ' Ghost' in this
particular instance.

## SUPPOSED HINTS OF THE TRINITY IN THE OLD TESTAMENT—THE WORD GOD.

If the Trinity has been found in the Old Testament, it has not been on account of errors in the original text, or to any great extent through mistranslations in the Authorized Version. The discovery has been possible only by means of forced applications of passages which to the writers themselves had no such meaning, and by imaginative inferences from mere peculiarities of Hebrew idioms and modes of thought. It was hardly to be expected, therefore, that a Revision of the Old Testament would throw much new light upon this subject.

One of the passages most relied upon to prove that the Trinity was at least implicitly revealed in the Old Testament (Is. xlviii. 16), will be better dealt with hereafter [see p. 51]. It will be seen in that instance that the Revision gives little countenance to the common view of the text in question. The few other texts often quoted to this effect will be found, very properly, unaltered in the Revised Version—such, for example, as Ps. xxxiii, 6, ' By the word of the Lord were the heavens made, and all the host of them by the breath of his mouth ;' and some persons may still imagine that the terms 'Lord, word and breath (or, *spirit*)' indicate a Divine Trinity, while others will, with better reason, think that 'the word of the Lord' and 'the breath of his mouth' rather mean the same thing, according to the rules of parallelism in Hebrew poetry. (See a similar passage in Is. xxxiv. 16.) The three-fold repetition of the term ' Holy' before the Divine name in such passages as Is. vi. 3, and of the name ' Jehovah' in the form of blessing in Num. vi. 24—26, which is supposed to imply a Trinity, will also be found, and of course without change, in the Revised Version. In such cases, there has been no question of either readings or renderings. Unitarians may still say, as they have always said, that the Trinitarian inference from these very simple and natural Oriental forms of expression is unwarranted and unreasonable.

But it has been believed that among what Canon Liddon calls the 'occult references' to this doctrine, the 'plural form' of the Divine name 'was necessary' to be used by Moses with a verb in the singular in the very first verse of the Bible, 'in order to hint at the complex mystery of God's inner life,'[1] the text reading, 'In the beginning God (literally 'gods') created (literally 'he created') the heavens and the earth.' It will be interesting, therefore, to note the changes made or suggested in the Revised Version in certain passages in which the word Elohim, the plural name of God, occurs.

### GEN. iii. 5.

| *Authorized Version.* | *Revised Version.* |
|---|---|
| Then your eyes shall be opened, and ye shall be as gods, knowing good and evil. | Then your eyes shall be opened, and ye shall be as God,* knowing good and evil. [* Or, *gods.* |

So Mr. Wellbeloved translated, 'Ye will be as God,' since the first pair could have known only the one God with whom they were in communication.

### Ex. xxxii. 1, 4.

| | |
|---|---|
| Make us gods which shall go before us. | Make us gods* which shall go before us. [* Or, *a god.* |
| 4. And they said, These be thy gods, O Israel, which brought thee up out of the land of Egypt. And when Aaron saw *it*, he built an altar before it. | 4. And they said, These be thy gods,* O Israel, which brought thee up out of the land of Egypt. And when Aaron saw *this*, he built an altar before it. [* Or, *this is thy god.* |

This is also Mr. Wellbeloved's translation, the calf being

---

[1] Bampton Lectures, 1866, Lect. II. It should be noted, by the way, that the plural word is applied to Moses himself in Ex. vii. 1: 'See, I have made thee a god (Elohim) to Pharaoh.' The expression is the same, and it is used in the same manner, in such passages as Ps. lxxxvi. 10: 'Thou art God (Elohim) alone.'

single, though the Hebrew word is as usual in the plural. So the incident is described in Neh. ix. 18, 'This is thy God,' viz. the molten calf.

### 1 SAM. xxviii. 13.

| *Authorized Version.* | *Revised Version.* |
|---|---|
| And the woman said unto Saul, I saw gods ascending out of the earth; and he said unto her, What form is he of? | And the woman said unto Saul, I see a god* coming up out of the earth; and he said unto her, What form is he of?<br>[* Or, *gods*. |

Dr. G. Vance Smith translates, with the Revisers, 'a god,' since the preternatural figure so denominated was clearly one, not many,—the figure of the old, departed prophet, Samuel. The Revisers might well have left out their marginal note, for the usage of the name in the plural for a supernatural being was well understood by the Hebrews.

---

In one of the Psalms the marginal note enables the ordinary reader to see how freely the term 'god' or 'gods' was used by the Hebrew writers—

### Ps. xxix. 1.

| Give unto the LORD, O ye mighty . . . glory and strength. | Give unto the LORD, O ye sons* of the mighty,† . . . glory and strength.<br>[* Or, *sons of God*. † Or, *gods*, see Ex. xv. 11. |

The Revisers insert the same notes in the margin at Ps. lxxxix. 6, 'Who among the sons of the mighty is like unto the LORD?'

Since the word which we translate 'God.' when it designates the Divine Being, occurs so commonly in the plural form, while it must sometimes be translated 'gods,' or 'mighty ones,' there is an occasional ambiguity which the context does not always give the means of clearing up. Thus in Josh. xxii. 22 the Revision reads: 'The Lord the God of gods, he knoweth,' but the marginal note is, 'or, *God, even*

*God the Lord,* Heb. *El Elohim, Jehovah.*' In Ps. l. 1, however, the same words are translated differently, and for the
Authorized 'The mighty God, even the Lord,' the Revision
reads in the text what is put in the other passage in the
margin, 'God, even God the Lord.'

There is no doubt that, as suggested in the text above
cited, the plural Elohim was sometimes used with a plural
sense to designate rulers, mighty men, especially the chief
men of Israel, as well as the gods of the nations.   Jesus
argued (John x. 34) from this familiar usage, in justification of his claim to be *a* Son of God (so it stands in the
Greek, as the Revisers indicate by putting the definite article,
which they adopt, in italics).   The passage he referred to
occurs in Ps. lxxxii. 6, 'I said, ye are gods, and all of you
sons of the Most High' (R. V.).   In the opening of the
Psalm the Revisers translate, 'God standeth in the congregation of God,' where the Authorized Version had, 'the
congregation of the mighty.'   They also say, Ex. xxii. 28,
'Thou shalt not revile God (putting ' or, *the judges,*' of the
Authorized Version in the margin), nor curse a ruler of thy
people.'   They make the same change also in several other
places.   In Ex. xxi. 6, where the Authorized Version says,
'they shall bring him to the judges,' the Revisers say 'to
God,' putting ' or, *the judges,*' in the margin, and the same in
xxii. 8, 9.   So in 1 Sam. ii. 25, 'the judge shall judge him,'
reads now 'God (Elohim),' ' or, *the judge,*' appearing in the
margin.   In 1 Chron. xxiv. 5, instead of 'governors of the
house of God,' we now read, 'princes of God.'

The same kind of change is made in the well-known
Psalm, which is quoted in Heb. ii. 7, from the Septuagint,
where Elohim was before translated 'angels'—

Ps. viii. 5.

| *Authorized Version.* | *Revised Version.* |
|---|---|
| For thou hast made him a little lower than the angels. | For thou hast made him but little lower than God.* |
| | [* Or, *the angels.* |

How the plural word Elohim was used with special reference to the One Divine Being may be seen in Deut. xxxii. 39, 'I am he, and there is no God (Elohim) with me;' also in Josh. xxiv. 19, where the Revisers had no improvement to suggest. Joshua says to the people, 'Ye cannot serve Jehovah, for he is a holy God,' both words, the adjective as well as the substantive, being in the plural, 'he is holy Gods,' if literally translated. They have, however, rightly corrected in several instances, adopting the same rule of interpretation :

### Hos. xi. 12.

| *Authorized Version.* | *Revised Version.* |
|---|---|
| But Judah yet ruleth with God, and is faithful with the saints. | But Judah yet ruleth with God, and is faithful with the Holy One. |

Which would be, if translated literally, 'the Holy Ones.' In the following passages also the same plural form occurs, which the Revisers, with Mr. Wellbeloved, understand to mean the One All-holy Being.

### Prov. xxx. 3. ·

| | |
|---|---|
| I neither learned wisdom, nor have I the knowledge of the holy. | And I have not learned wisdom, neither have I* the knowledge of the Holy One. |
| | [* Or, *that I should have the knowledge of the Holy One.* |

### Prov. ix. 10.

| | |
|---|---|
| The fear of the LORD is the beginning of wisdom, and the knowledge of the holy is understanding. | The fear of the LORD is the beginning of wisdom, and the knowledge of the Holy One is understanding. |

The Revisers are probably right in all these cases, considering the parallelism, since the literal translation would obviously imply plain polytheism.

## THE SOLE DEITY AND UNITY OF GOD.

Though it may be regretted that the Revisers, while they explain in the notes that Jehovah is the Hebrew proper name which in the Old Testament they render LORD, have not introduced it everywhere in the text, yet the force and value of their admission should not be unappreciated.  At the passage where this name first occurs (JHVH, Gen. ii. 4), they note thus in the margin: 'Heb. Jehovah, as in other places where LORD is put in capitals.'  The American Revisers urged a bolder and more intelligible course.  They say, Substitute the Divine name Jehovah, wherever it occurs in the Hebrew text, for 'the LORD' and 'God.'[1]  The passage referred to would then read, 'in the day that Jehovah God

---

[1] The Revisers have done this in two instances, which show how great the improvement would have been if the American suggestion had been adopted throughout the Old Testament.

### Ex. vi. 2.

| *Authorized Version.* | *Revised Version.* |
|---|---|
| And God spake unto Moses, and said unto him, I am the LORD: and I appeared unto Abraham, unto Isaac, and unto Jacob, by *the name of* God Almighty, but by my name JEHOVAH was I not known to them. | And God spake unto Moses, and said unto him, I am JEHOVAH; and I appeared unto Abraham, unto Isaac, and unto Jacob, as God Almighty,* but by† my name JEHOVAH I was not known‡ to them.<br><br>[* Heb. *El Shaddai.*    † Or, *as to.*    ‡ Or, *made known.* |

### HAB. iii. 19.

| The LORD God is my strength. | Jehovah, the Lord, is my strength. |
|---|---|

It is curious to note in the context of the passage from Exodus the incongruity created by the sudden change back to the Authorized 'LORD' after the improvement in *vv.* 7 and 8, where the phrase is repeated, 'I am Jehovah.'  In *v.* 10 the Version goes on, 'And the Lord,' &c., altogether ignoring the preceding express declaration of the Divine Name.

made earth and heaven,' the proper name being given instead
of 'the LORD' of the Septuagint translators, which, besides
creating frequent ambiguities in the Old Testament, has
caused an almost hopeless confusion in many places of the
New Testament, the quotations in which are mostly made,
not from the Hebrew, but from their Greek version.   There
may have been some difficulty with regard to the proper
method of representing in English the vowels of the Hebrew
name, the form Jehovah being admittedly incorrect, but had
this familiar word been used instead of the misleading term
LORD, it would probably have prepared the way for a future
more correct expression.

In the following three passages, the Revision brings out
more clearly the Unity of God as identified with the One
Personal Name which always represented that doctrine to
the Jewish people.   Comparing them as they stand side by
side, it will become evident how much the ordinary reader
would gain in the intelligent reading of the Old Testament by
substituting the proper name for the vague and ambiguous
term of the Greek version.   It is a clear advantage for him
to be made aware that this *may* (the American company
say *should*) be done throughout the Old Testament—

### ZECH. xiv. 9.

| *Authorized Version.* | *Revised Version.* |
|---|---|
| And the LORD shall be King over all the earth: in that day shall there be one LORD, and his name one. | And the LORD shall be King over all the earth: in that day shall the LORD be one, and his name one. |

### Ps. lxiii. 18.

| | |
|---|---|
| That men may know that thou, whose name alone is Jehovah, art the Most High over all the earth. | That they may know that thou alone,* whose name is Jehovah, art the Most High over all the earth.<br><br>[* Or, *thou whose name alone is.* |

## NEH. ix. 6.

| *Authorized Version.* | *Revised Version.* |
|---|---|
| Thou, even thou, art LORD alone, thou hast made heaven, &c. | Thou art the LORD, even thou alone, thou hast made heaven, &c. |

---

### *The Unity of God as set forth in the New Testament.*

## ROM. iii. 29, 30.

| Is he the God of the Jews only? is he not also of the Gentiles? Yes, of the Gentiles also; seeing it is one God which shall justify, &c. | Or is God *the God* of Jews only? is he not the God of Gentiles also? Yea, of Gentiles also; if so be that God is one, and he shall justify, &c. |
|---|---|

The Improved Version also had the correction, 'Is God the God of Jews,' &c., keeping clear of the idea of national or many gods, which was certainly not the idea in Paul's mind; and the further change from 'it is one,' to 'there is one God;' but that Version had nothing so emphatically Unitarian as the Revised, 'if so be that God is one,' which is indeed the turning-point of the argument.

---

## MARK xii. 29, 30, 32.

| And Jesus answered him, The first of all the commandments is, Hear, O Israel, the Lord our God is one Lord, and thou shalt love the Lord thy God . . .<br><br>v. 32. And the Scribe said unto him, Well, Master, thou hast said the truth: for there is one God, and there is none other but he. | Jesus answered, The first is, Hear, O Israel; the Lord our God,* the Lord is one; and thou shalt love the Lord thy God.<br><br>v. 32. And the Scribe said unto him, Of a truth, Master,† thou hast well said that he is one; and there is none other but he.<br><br>[* Or, *is our God.*  † Or, *Teacher.* |
|---|---|

The Improved Version has here the alternative form given

THE UNITY OF GOD.

in the margin, 'The Lord is our God, the Lord is one.' In
Deut. vi. 4, from which the text was quoted, the Revisers
follow the Common Version, but they place in the margin
three alternative translations, the one given by the New Testament Revisers, that of the Improved Version, and a third,
which could not be got out of the original words in Mark,
viz. 'The Lord is our God, the Lord alone.' Mr. Sharpe,
however, adopts it in the original passage, 'Jehovah is our
God, Jehovah alone.' In the 32nd verse here the Improved
Version led the way : 'In truth, Master, thou hast said well
that he is one, and there is none other but he.' It would
be difficult to put the Unitarian view of God into a more
precise statement. On the supposition of three Personalities of any kind in the Divine Nature, it would have been
at least more natural to say 'that *they* are one, and there is
none other but they.'

MATT. xix. 17.

| *Authorized Version.* | *Revised Version.* |
|---|---|
| And he said unto him, Why callest thou me good? There is none good but one, *that is,* God. | And he said unto him, Why askest thou me concerning that which is good?* One there is who is good.<br><br>[* Some ancient authorities read, *Why callest thou me good? None is good save one, even God.* See Mark x. 18; Luke xviii. 19. |

In this correction there would seem little ground left for
the orthodox implication that Jesus was here in reality re-
buking the inquirer for attributing to him a quality belonging
only to God, while yet he simply looked upon him as a
human being. The affirmation is the same, however, in the
three Gospels, that there is but one All-perfect Being, one
only supremely good.

In the following passage, the personal Unity of God is

well distinguished from his sole Deity, the idea expressed in the Authorized Version, which the Revisers have relegated to the margin.   Here also the Improved Version was before them, making the same correction—

### JAMES ii. 19.

| *Authorized Version.* | *Revised Version.* |
| --- | --- |
| Thou believest that there is one God ; thou doest well. | Thou believest that God is one ;* thou doest well. |
|  | [* Some ancient authorities read, *there is one God.* |

When the New Testament writers wish to speak of the sole Deity, of God as God alone, they use different language, as in the passages following, in which, moreover, in the Revised Version the Deity of the one only God is more distinctly indicated:

### 1 TIM. i. 17.

| Now unto the King eternal, immortal, invisible, the only wise God, be honour and glory. | Now unto the King eternal, incorruptible, invisible, the only God, be honour and glory. |
| --- | --- |

This was the reading of the Improved Version, adopting the text of Griesbach.   Happily the phrase, 'the only wise God,' no longer admitted here, does not drop out of the New Testament.   It occurs in a more suitable connection in Rom. xvi. 27.[1]   In a doxology the writer naturally dwells

---

[1] In that passage, which reads in the Authorized Version, 'to God only wise be glory through Jesus Christ for ever,' the Revision presents what may at first seem a radical and orthodox alteration.   'To the only wise God, through Jesus Christ, to whom (Marg. some ancient authorities omit 'to whom') be the glory for ever.'   But any mistake as to the object of this ascription of praise is one hardly likely to be made by the most ordinary reader, or if it were possibly suggested, the remark of Dean Alford's gives ample reason for a more rational interpretation: 'The "to whom" cannot without great harshness be referred to Christ, seeing that the words, "to the only wise God," resume the chief subject

upon the majesty of the sole Eternal One. The same correction was made also from Griesbach in the Improved Version in the next passage, in which too was the same addition as is here introduced. The effect of this addition, 'through Jesus Christ our Lord,' is obviously to make it more clear that the Father is meant by ' the only God our Saviour,' and the Father only—

## JUDE 25.

| *Authorized Version.* | *Revised Version.* |
|---|---|
| To the only wise God our Saviour be glory and majesty, dominion and power, now and for ever. | To the only God our Saviour, through Jesus Christ our Lord, be glory, majesty, dominion and power, before all time, and now, and for evermore.* |
| | [* Gr. *unto all the ages.* |

## JOHN v. 44.

| | |
|---|---|
| How can ye believe which receive honour one of another, and seek not the honour that cometh from God only? | How can ye believe which receive glory one of another, and the glory that *cometh* from the only God ye seek not? |

The Improved Version renders this, 'from the only God.' The Revisers note in the margin that ' some ancient authorities read, the only One.' The mistranslation of the Greek in the Authorized Version was, as Dr. G. Vance Smith observes,[1] an extraordinary one. The remarkable fact here is that these are words attributed to Jesus himself, and by the author of the Proem to this Gospel.

---

of the sentence, and to them the relative pronoun must apply.' There is a similar construction in Heb. xiii. 21, where as it is a doxology there could not possibly be any real ambiguity. See also 1 Pet. iv. 11, where the sense is equally beyond question, if only for the same reason.

[1] Texts and Margins of the Revised New Testament affecting Theological Doctrine briefly Reviewed, by G. Vance Smith, B.A., &c., p. 22.

## GOD SPECIFICALLY NAMED THE FATHER.

In the six important passages below, the Revisers follow the course of the Improved Version in amending the somewhat pointless, not to say ambiguous, phrase of the Common Version, 'God and our Father,' and emphasize the fact that by 'our God' and 'our Father' the same Divine Personality is meant, the Being indeed of whom Jesus often speaks as God our 'Heavenly Father'—

### JAMES i. 27.

| *Authorized Version.* | *Revised Version.* |
|---|---|
| Pure religion and undefiled before God and the Father is this, to visit the fatherless, &c. | Pure religion and undefiled before our God and Father is this, to visit the fatherless, &c. |

### PHIL. iv. 20.

| | |
|---|---|
| Now unto God and our Father be glory for ever and ever. | Now unto our God and Father be the glory for ever and ever. |

### GAL. i. 3—5.

| | |
|---|---|
| Grace be to you and peace, from God the Father, and from our Lord Jesus Christ, who gave himself for our sins, that he might deliver us from this present evil world, according to the will of God and our Father, to whom be glory for ever and ever. | Grace to you and peace from God the Father,* and our Lord Jesus Christ, who gave himself for our sins, that he might deliver us out of this present evil world,† according to the will of our God and Father: to whom be the glory for ever and ever. |

[* Some ancient authorities read, *from God our Father and the Lord Jesus Christ.*   † Or, *age.*

## 1 THES. i. 2—4.

| *Authorized Version.* | *Revised Version.* |
|---|---|
| We give thanks to God always for you all ... remembering ... your patience of hope in our Lord Jesus Christ, in the sight of God and our Father; knowing, brethren beloved, your election of God. | We give thanks to God always for you all ... remembering ... your patience of hope in our Lord Jesus Christ, before our God and Father; knowing, brethren beloved of God, your election. [The Improved Version has this further correction also.] |

## 1 THES. iii. 11—13.

| | |
|---|---|
| Now God himself and our Father, and our Lord Jesus Christ, direct our way unto you. And the Lord make you to increase and abound in love ... to the end he may stablish your hearts unblamable in holiness before God even our Father, at the coming of our Lord Jesus Christ with all his saints. | Now may our God and Father himself, and our Lord Jesus, direct our way unto you; and the Lord make you to increase and abound in love ... to the end he may stablish your hearts unblamable in holiness before our God and Father, at the coming of our Lord Jesus with all his saints. |

## COL. iii. 17.

| | |
|---|---|
| And whatsoever ye do in word or deed, *do* all in the name of the Lord Jesus, giving thanks to God and the Father by him. | And whatsoever ye do in word or in deed, *do* all in the name of the Lord Jesus, giving thanks to God the Father through him. |

It is thus made clear that God, in the New Testament, means the Father only, not the first of several persons, as theologians use the term. God is the Father, and the Father the one God: the words are synonymous. This is expessed in another way in Eph. v. 20, 'to God, even the Father,' the corresponding text to the one just cited. The Improved Version so translates in both instances. The phrase is not a new one, nor peculiar to the Revised Version; the Authorizcd has it in 1 Cor. xv. 24, 'When he shall have delivered up the kingdom to God, even the Father,' or, as we might say, 'to God, that is, the Father.' The identity of the two terms appears very plainly in the passage next quoted in the words of Jesus himself. The Revision brings out the sense in the most pointed manner. In the Improved Version it was, 'him hath the Father sealed, even God'—

## JOHN vi. 27.

| *Authorized Version.* | *Revised Version.* |
|---|---|
| That meat which endureth unto everlasting life, which the Son of Man shall give unto you: for him hath God the Father sealed. | The meat which abideth unto eternal life, which the Son of Man shall give unto you: for him the Father, *even* God, hath sealed. |

## THE FATHER THE GOD OF JESUS ALSO.

### 2 COR. i. 3.

| *Authorized Version.* | *Revised Version.* |
|---|---|
| Blessed be God, even the Father of our Lord Jesus Christ, the Father of mercies, and the God of all comfort. | Blessed be the God and Father of our Lord Jesus Christ, the Father of mercies and God of all comfort. |

### ROM. xv. 5, 6.

| | |
|---|---|
| Now the God of patience and consolation grant you to be likeminded one towards another, according to (marg. *after the example of*) Christ Jesus ; that ye may with one mind and one mouth glorify God, even the Father of our Lord Jesus Christ. | Now the God of patience and of comfort grant you to be of the same mind one with another, according to Christ Jesus ; that with one accord ye may with one mouth glorify the God and Father of our Lord Jesus Christ. |

On the former of these passages Mr. Sharpe makes a quaint remark which may apply to both : ' King James' translators did not like to call the Almighty the God of Jesus Christ, although Jesus himself expressly so styles the Father in John xx. 17, I ascend unto my Father and your Father, and my God and your God ;' and although further, he might have added, they in another passage, Eph. i. 17, did translate, having no alternative, ' That the God of our Lord Jesus Christ, the Father of glory, may give unto you a spirit of wisdom,' &c. ' Here openly,' says Erasmus, ' the Father is called the God of Jesus Christ, which in other texts was ambiguous.' In both the texts above given, the Revisers were anticipated in the Improved Version, which reads, ' the God and Father of our Lord Jesus Christ.' His own exclamation on the cross will occur to the reader, the opening words of the 22nd Psalm, ' My God, my God, why hast thou forsaken me ?'

D 2

The Revised Version has one text less in which God is
named the Father of Christ; but the advantage gained is
obvious, in that it is now made clear that the writer intended
to say that the family is named from the father, a play upon
the two Greek words, one of which is derived from the other;
and that he is not here speaking of the headship of the
Church in Christ, as the Authorized Version might have
been understood to imply.  'From whom' obviously refers
to the Father—

EPH. iii. 14, 15.

| *Authorized Version.* | *Revised Version.* |
|---|---|
| I bow my knees unto the Father of our Lord Jesus Christ, of whom the whole family in heaven and earth is named. | I bow my knees unto the Father, from whom every family* in heaven and earth is named.<br><br>[* Gr. *fatherhood.* |

In the two following passages the Revised Version brings
out the true relationship between Christ and the Almighty
still more markedly, after the example, in both cases, of the
Improved Version :

REV. iii. 2.

| For I have not found thy works perfect before God. | For I have found* no works of thine fulfilled before my God.<br><br>[* Many ancient authorities read, *not found thy works.* |
|---|---|

REV. i. 6.

| And hath made us Kings and Priests unto God and his Father. | And he made us to be a kingdom, to be priests unto his God and Father. |
|---|---|

How little ground, therefore, could there have been for
the foolish inference of the Jews, in John v. 18, that Jesus
made himself equal with God by simply affirming that God
was his Father.   The true point is well brought out by the
Revised correction, 'his own Father.'   He had, in fact,
realized for himself what to them had been only a pious
phrase.

## THE HOLY SPIRIT, THE SPIRIT OF GOD.

The term 'Spirit of God' is often equivalent in Scripture usage to the Divine Being himself, or to his power and wisdom, but more commonly it is employed to express special influence or power imparted by God to men. In the following passage, Paul bases an argument for the inspired truth of the spiritual consciousness in the Christian believer upon the fact that it comes first-hand from the Spirit of God, comparing this Spirit with the self-conscious Spirit in man ; and so he brings the two conceptions together,—of the Divine Mind in itself, and of its communication to men ; first of the Spirit as God knowing perfectly his own thought and purposes, and secondly of the same Spirit imparted as a gift of spiritual insight, an intercommunion of the divine with the human consciousness. The changes made here in the Revision will appear slight, but they help to bring out the sense more forcibly—

I COR. ii. 10—13.

| *Authorized Version.* | *Revised Version.* |
|---|---|
| But God hath revealed *them* unto us by his Spirit: for the Spirit searcheth all things, yea, the deep things of God. For what man knoweth the things of a man, save the spirit of man which is in him? Even so the things of God knoweth no man, but the spirit of God. Now we have received, not the spirit of the world, but the spirit which is of God, that we might know the things that are freely | But unto us God revealed *them*\* through the Spirit: for the Spirit searcheth all things, yea, the deep things of God. For who among men knoweth the things of a man, save the spirit of the man which is in him? even so the things of God none knoweth, save the Spirit of God. But we received, not the spirit of the world, but the spirit which is of God ; that we might know the things that |

[\* Or, *it* (i.e. the wisdom of God above referred to.

| *Authorized Version.* | *Revised Version.* |
|---|---|
| given to us of God. Which things also we speak, not in the words which man's wisdom teacheth, but which the Holy Ghost teacheth. | are freely given to us by God. Which things also we speak, not in words which man's wisdom teacheth, but which the Spirit teacheth. |

In writing to the Romans, Paul represents the matter from another point of view, with still the same idea present to his thought of the Divine in intercommunion with the human spirit. God the Spirit knows what is in his own mind, and therefore it is divine truth which the imparted Spirit of God reveals. This is what the Apostle says in the text just quoted. He now reasons in the reverse direction, that the mind of the Spirit as a power of spiritual life in man is known to the Giver of that holy influence, which must needs move in harmony with his will, because it is his own Spirit present in the souls of the faithful. The passage is the more noteworthy as being one of the few in which the Revisers have introduced an expression as of distinct personality of the Spirit, beyond what appears in the Authorized Version. Their capitals also are significant in the other texts cited—

## ROM. viii. 26, 27.

| | |
|---|---|
| Likewise the Spirit also helpeth our infirmities: for we know not what we should pray for as we ought: but the Spirit itself maketh intercession for us with groanings which cannot be uttered [alluding to the 23rd verse, *but ourselves also, which have the firstfruits of the Spirit, even we ourselves groan within ourselves*]. | And in like manner the Spirit also helpeth our infirmity: for we know not how to pray as we ought: but the Spirit himself maketh intercession for us with groanings which cannot be uttered. |
| And he that searcheth the hearts knoweth what is the | And he that searcheth the hearts knoweth what is the |

| *Authorized Version.* | *Revised Version.* |
|---|---|
| mind of the Spirit, because he maketh intercession for the saints according to the will of God. | mind of the Spirit, because he maketh intercession for the saints according to the will of God. |

The word 'Spirit' being in Greek neuter, there was no grammatical reason for the Authorized '*he* maketh' in ver. 27, neither was there for the Revised 'the Spirit *himself*' in ver. 26; and the same remark applies to a previous verse (16), in which 'the Spirit itself' is altered, as in the 26th verse, to 'the Spirit himself.' But it makes little difference whether the pronoun be 'he' or 'it,' since it is clear from other passages in Paul's writings that his idea was, that God was present in the power of his own very Spirit in the Christian mind and heart; as, for example, 1 Cor. iii. 16, 'Know ye not that ye are a temple of God, and that the Spirit of God dwelleth in you?' See also 1 Cor. vi. 19, 'Or know ye not that your body is a temple (marg. or, *sanctuary*) of the Holy Ghost (marg. or, *Holy Spirit*) which is in you, which ye have from God?' The same conception appears in the following passages, with amendments made or suggested in regard to the designation of the Divine presence and power:

### 1 JOHN iii. 24.

| And he that keepeth his commandments dwelleth in him, and he in him: and hereby we know that he abideth in us, by the spirit which he hath given us. | And he that keepeth his commandments abideth in him, and he in him. And hereby we know that he abideth in us, by the Spirit which he hath given us. |
|---|---|

### 2 TIM. i. 13.

| That good thing which was committed unto thee, keep, by the Holy Ghost which dwelleth in us. | That good thing which was committed unto thee guard through the Holy Ghost* which dwelleth in us. |
|---|---|
| | [* Or, *Holy Spirit*. |

In the margin at John iv. 24 occurs a note that should not be overlooked.  Instead of 'God is a Spirit,' the Revisers intimate may be read, 'God is spirit.'  This may prove the proper translation if the context is considered.  Jesus meant to say that God was not a local Divinity, to be honoured in one place and not in another; but also that being spirit, not material, he must be spiritually worshipped, not in mere outward forms.  He was not giving a definition of the Divine Nature, otherwise it would be obvious to remark that we cannot conceive of a Spirit divided into three Personalities. Each of three Persons in any Divine Trinity, the first and second as well as the third, must of course be a Spirit also.

---

The Revisers, especially the Revisers of the Old Testament, endeavour by the use of capitals and small letters to distinguish between 'the spirit' as indicating the mind or the power or other attribute of God, and 'the Spirit' as a term of personality.   Hence their mode of expression in the following passage (which, moreover, clearly illustrates the text above from 1 Cor. ii. 10, 11, p. 37)—

Is. xl. 13.

*Authorized Version.*

Who hath directed the Spirit of the LORD, or being his counsellor hath taught him?

*Revised Version.*

Who hath directed* the spirit of the LORD, or being his counsellor hath taught him?

[* Or, *meted out.*

Where 'the spirit' is manifestly 'the mind' of the Lord, the expression which Paul uses.  Dr. Noyes (1865) translates it, 'Who hath searched out the spirit of Jehovah,' which is probably correct, as the Revised margin also suggests, 'meted out' being the phrase used just before.  Paul quotes the passage twice from the Septuagint in this sense (Rom. xi. 34 and 1 Cor. ii. 16), 'Who hath known the mind of the Lord?'

The use of the word 'spirit' for 'mind' may be noted in one of the Revised suggestions of amendment in the margin. David is giving his parting directions to Solomon for the building of the Temple:

1 CHRON. xxviii. 12.

| Authorized Version. | Revised Version. |
|---|---|
| And the pattern of all that he had by the spirit of the courts of the house of the Lord. | And the pattern of all that he had by the spirit* for the courts of the house of the Lord.<br>[* Or, *in his spirit.* |

Mr. J. Scott Porter and Mr. S. Sharpe say plainly, 'of all that he had in his mind.' The dwelling of the Divine Spirit in man was not an idea peculiar to the Hebrews, but the reason for the following correction from 'Spirit' to 'spirit' is obvious, considering who is the speaker:

GEN. xli. 38.

| And Pharaoh said unto his servants, Can we find *such a one* as this *is*, a man in whom the Spirit of God *is?* | And Pharaoh said unto his servants, Can we find such a one as this, a man in whom the spirit of God is? |

Compare Dan. iv. 8, 'in whom is the spirit of the holy gods;' also Ex. xxxi. 3, 'And I have filled him with the spirit of God in wisdom . . . and in all manner of workmanship.' The Revisers make the same distinction in cases where 'the spirit of God' obviously means the Divine energy or wisdom, following generally, but not always, the method of the Authorized translators. Compare particularly the two following passages:

JOB xxxiii. 4.

| The Spirit of God hath made me, and the breath of the Almighty hath given me life. | The spirit of God hath made me, and the breath of the Almighty hath given me life. |

JOB xxvi. 13, 14.

| He divided the sea with his power, and by his understanding he smiteth through the | He stirreth up* the sea with his power, and by his understanding he smiteth through<br>[* Or, *stilleth.* |

| *Authorized Version.* | *Revised Version.* |
|---|---|
| proud.  By his spirit he hath garnished the heavens ; his hand hath formed the crooked serpent. | Rahab.  By his spirit the heavens are garnished,† his hand hath pierced the swift‡ serpent. |

[† Heb. *beauty*.   ‡ Or, *fleeing*, or, *gliding*.

### GEN. i. 2.

| And the Spirit of God moved upon the face of the waters. | And the spirit of God moved upon* the face of the waters. |
|---|---|

[* Or, *was brooding upon*.

Mr. Wellbeloved leaves the Authorized Version here as he found it, 'the Spirit of God,' noting that although the Hebrew word means primarily wind or breath, and the phrase would be perfectly well translated 'a mighty wind,' yet the verb seems rather to suggest the conception of the Divine Energy preparing itself to bring the original chaos into a cosmos.  Compare, however, with this :

### Is. xl. 7.

| The grass withereth, the flower fadeth ; because the spirit of the LORD bloweth upon it. | The grass withereth, the flower fadeth ; because the breath of the LORD bloweth upon it. |
|---|---|

---

Numerous passages occur in the Old Testament in which the Spirit of God is said to have been given, or put and poured out upon men, in which no distinction is made in the Authorized orthography, and in such cases no change is made in the Revision.  Here, however, are other examples which the Revisers correct :

### 1 SAM. xi. 6.

| And the Spirit of God came upon Saul when he heard those tidings, and his anger was kindled greatly. | And the spirit of God came mightily upon Saul when he heard those words, and his anger was kindled greatly. |
|---|---|

I SAM. xvi. 13, 14.

| *Authorized Version.* | *Revised Version.* |
| --- | --- |
| Then Samuel took the horn of oil, and anointed him in the midst of his brethren: and the Spirit of the LORD came upon David from that day forward. But the Spirit of the LORD departed from Saul, and an evil spirit from the Lord troubled him. | Then Samuel took the horn of oil, and anointed him in the midst of his brethren: and the spirit of the LORD came mightily upon David from that day forward. But the spirit of the LORD had departed from Saul, and an evil spirit from the Lord troubled him. |

See in the Psalm attributed to David (li. 11), 'Cast me not away from thy presence, and take not thy holy spirit from me.' It is remarkable that the two expressions, the presence and the spirit of God, are conjoined in the same manner in another Psalm (cxxxix. 7), 'Whither shall I go from thy spirit? or whither shall I flee from thy presence?'

———

In about a dozen other places in the Old Testament the spirit of God, or of the Lord, is presented in the same form as in the texts given above, and in each case the Revisers use small letters to indicate that the reference is to some power or gift, not to the Divine Personal Agency. The following is a remarkable illustration of another use of the term : 'The hand of the LORD was upon me, and he carried me out in the spirit of the LORD, and set me down in the midst of the valley' (Ezek. xxxvii. 1). The New Testament Revisers follow the Authorized Version in using a capital 'S' in the similar passage in Acts viii. 39, 40 : 'When they were come up out of the water, the Spirit of the Lord caught away Philip . . . but Philip was found at Azotus,' &c.

Some of the passages in which the Revisers have made the change referred to, throw a singular light upon the old Hebrew conception of the Spirit—

## JUDGES xiv. 6.

| *Authorized Version.* | *Revised Version.* |
| --- | --- |
| And, behold, a young lion roared against him [Samson]. And the Spirit of the LORD came mightily upon him, and he rent him as he would have rent a kid. | And, behold, a young lion roared against him. And the spirit of the LORD came mightily upon him, and he rent him as he would have rent a kid. |

## JUDGES xiv. 19.

| | |
| --- | --- |
| And the Spirit of the LORD came upon him, and he went down to Ashkelon, and slew thirty men of them. | And the spirit of the LORD came mightily upon him, and he went down to Ashkelon, and smote thirty men of them. |

## 1 KINGS xxii. 24, also 2 CHRON. xviii. 23.

| | |
| --- | --- |
| Zedekiah . . . went near, and smote Micaiah on the cheek, and said, Which way went the Spirit of the LORD from me to speak unto thee? | Then Zedekiah . . . . came near, and smote Micaiah on the cheek, and said, Which way went the spirit of the LORD from me to speak unto thee? |

---

There is a fine prophetic passage in which the Revisers follow the rule above indicated, and which at the same time shows how familiar to the Hebrew mind was the idea of the holy Spirit of God moving in and inspiring human souls.

## Is. lxiii. 10—12, 14.

| | |
| --- | --- |
| But they rebelled, and vexed his holy Spirit: therefore he was turned to be their enemy, and he fought against them. Then he remembered the days of old, Moses and his people, *saying*, Where is he that brought them up out of the sea with the | But they rebelled, and grieved his holy spirit: therefore he was turned to be their enemy, and himself fought against them. Then he remembered* the days of old, Moses, and his people, *saying*, Where is he that brought them up out of the sea with the |
| | [* Or, *then his people remembered the ancient days of Moses.* |

*Authorized Version.*

shepherd of his flock? Where is he that put his holy Spirit within him? That led them by the right hand of Moses with his glorious arm, dividing the water before them, to make himself an everlasting name? That led them through the deep, as an horse in the wilderness, that they should not stumble? As a beast goeth down into the valley, the Spirit of the LORD caused him to rest; so didst thou lead thy people, to make thyself a glorious name.

*Revised Version.*

shepherds† of his flock? where is he that put his holy spirit in the midst of them? that caused his glorious arm to go at the right hand of Moses? that divided the water before them, to make himself an everlasting name? that led them through the depths as an horse in the wilderness that they stumbled not? As the cattle that go down into the valley, the spirit of the LORD caused them to rest: so didst thou lead thy people, to make thyself a glorious name.

[† Another reading is, *shepherd.*

In this stirring appeal and recital of ancient story, the correction of a single letter in the Revised Version suggests the natural interpretation of 'his holy spirit' as referring to God himself, as in a corresponding text in Ps. lxxviii. 40. 'How oft did they rebel against him in the wilderness, and grieve him in the desert!' while the idea of the imparted spirit as a spirit of power and wisdom grows out of this, God's own spirit becoming an inspiration given to Moses, and through him directing and supporting his people.

The passage is the more interesting as bearing upon one in the New Testament in which the Revisers have introduced an idea of personality that does not appear in the Authorized Version:

### EPH. iv. 30.

And grieve not the holy Spirit of God, whereby ye are sealed unto the day of redemption.

And grieve not the Holy Spirit of God, in whom ye were sealed unto the day of redemption.

The correction may be right, though the Greek does not require it. The conception of grieving the Divine Being comes at all events nearer to the sense of the prophetic passage which the writer had evidently in his mind. It should be added that the further marginal amendments in that passage are very much in the line of Dr. G. V. Smith's version in the Revised Translation of 1862. Another striking illustration of the New Testament view of the fact alluded to by the prophet is seen in Stephen's denunciation of the Jewish council, 'Ye do always resist the Holy Spirit: as your fathers did, so do ye' (Acts vii. 51).

The following text still further illustrates this resisting of the Spirit of God:

### MATT. xii. 31.

| *Authorized Version.* | *Revised Version.* |
|---|---|
| But the blasphemy against the *holy* Ghost shall not be forgiven unto men. | But the blasphemy against the Spirit shall not be forgiven. |
| 32. But whosoever speaketh against the holy Ghost, it shall not be forgiven him. | 32. But whosoever shall speak against the Holy Spirit, it shall not be forgiven him. |

The change from 'Ghost' to 'Spirit' is made also in the parallel texts, Mark iii. 29, Luke xii. 10. In the present instance, the adjective 'holy' not being in the original, the Authorized Version inserted it in italics, since it was clearly impossible to translate, 'the blasphemy against the Ghost.' The Revisers avoid the difficulty by using the alternative word, 'the Spirit.' The difficulty is met in the same manner in John vii. 39 and 1 Cor. ii. 13 (see pp. 54, 49).

It is instructive to notice the score of passages in which, as here, the Revisers change the word 'Ghost' into 'Spirit.' In about sixty places it is retained, with both the words, 'Holy' and 'Ghost,' printed with the first letters in capitals. In one text (Rom. xv. 19), where the Authorized Version reads, 'by the power of the Spirit of God,' the Revisers have introduced instead the other term usually employed by them when the word 'Holy' precedes, 'in the power of the Holy

Ghost;' remarking, however, in the margin that 'many ancient authorities read *the Spirit of God;* one reads *the Spirit.*'

There is no difficulty in discovering in each instance of the change from Ghost to Spirit, something in the context that facilitated the correction, and in certain cases made it almost imperative. It appears that the American Revision Company would have preferred that the course should have been taken which was adopted in the Improved Version. One of their recommendations is, For ' Holy Ghost' adopt uniformly the rendering ' Holy Spirit.' The English Revisers have generally put the correction in the margin, as an alternative translation, in every book of the New Testament where the expression occurs. It is not found in Galatians, Ephesians, Philippians, Colossians, 2 Thessalonians, 1 Timothy, Philemon, James, 1, 2, and 3 John, and Revelation ; but only an equivalent form, the Spirit, or the Spirit of God, in a few places. The method adopted by the Revisers has been, in all cases where the words occur more than once or twice in a book, to say in the margin, when ' the Holy Ghost' first occurs : ' or, *Holy Spirit,* and so throughout this book.' The following examples may be specially noted, if only as showing the free use which has been made of the margin by the Revisers, and the importance of keeping it constantly in view in the reading of their Version :

MATT. i. 18, 20.

| *Authorized Version.* | *Revised Version.* |
|---|---|
| She was found with child of the Holy Ghost. | She was found with child of the Holy Ghost.* |
| That which is conceived in her is of the Holy Ghost. | That which is conceived† in her is of the Holy Ghost.* |
| | [* Or, *Holy Spirit.*    † Gr. *begotten.* |

It has been very properly pointed out in these verses, as also in Luke i. 35, 'the Holy Ghost shall come upon thee,' that besides the correction ' Holy Spirit' in the margin, it is

clearly better that the English definite article should not
introduce here the idea of a Personality in the Godhead of
which neither Joseph nor Mary could have had any previous
knowledge. They would naturally understand the promise
to be a promise of a divine influence, what Luke designates
'a power of the Most High.' (There is no article in the Greek.)

The same kind of reasoning has evidently led to the marginal note on Luke ii. 11, 'A Saviour which is Christ the
Lord,' margin 'or, *anointed Lord*,' there being no articles in
the original to indicate that this was a proper name.

### ACTS i. 2.

| *Authorized Version.* | *Revised Version.* |
|---|---|
| After that he [Jesus] through the Holy Ghost had given commandments unto the Apostles. | After that he had given commandment through the Holy Ghost* unto the apostles.<br><br>[* Or, *Holy Spirit.* |

### ACTS xi. 16.

| | |
|---|---|
| Then remembered I the word of the Lord, how that he said, John indeed baptized with water, but ye shall be baptized with the Holy Ghost. | And I remembered the word of the Lord, how that he said, John indeed baptized with water, but ye shall be baptized with* the Holy Ghost.†<br><br>[* Or, *in.*  † Or, *Holy Spirit.* See marg. i. 8. |

### ACTS v. 32.

| | |
|---|---|
| And we are his witnesses of these things, and so also is the Holy Ghost, whom God hath given to them that obey him. | And we are witnesses of these things, and so is the Holy Ghost,* whom God hath given to them that obey him.<br><br>[* Or, *Holy Spirit.* See marg. i. 2. |

Neither the Authorized translators nor the Revisers appear
to have observed the strangeness of the thought that God
could have granted to men a Divine personality as a gift,
the third subsistence in his own Eternal Being. The pronoun here in the Greek is not masculine, but neuter, as
agreeing in gender with the word which they translate 'Ghost.'

The Improved Version reads, 'and so is the holy spirit also, which God hath given to those that obey him.'

### ROM. v. 5.

| *Authorized Version.* | *Revised Version.* |
|---|---|
| And hope maketh not ashamed, because the love of God is shed abroad in our hearts, by the Holy Ghost, which is given us. | And hope putteth not to shame, because the love of God hath been shed abroad in our hearts through the Holy Ghost* which was given unto us.<br><br>[* Or, *Holy Spirit.* |

The change from 'by' to 'through' makes it clear that the writer had in his mind the idea of a Divine influence. This becomes express inspiration in the texts following:

### MARK xiii. 11.

| | |
|---|---|
| For it is not ye that speak, but the Holy Ghost. | For it is not ye that speak, but the Holy Ghost.*<br><br>[* Or, *Holy Spirit*, see Mark i. 8, margin. |

### LUKE xii. 12.

| | |
|---|---|
| For the Holy Ghost shall teach you in the same hour what ye ought to say. | For the Holy Spirit shall teach you in that very hour what ye ought to say. |

The change is made here in the text probably because the Holy Spirit had been just before mentioned. Besides, in the corresponding passage in Matt. x. 20, Jesus says, 'It is not ye that speak, but the Spirit of your Father that speaketh in you.'

### I COR. ii. 13.

| | |
|---|---|
| Not in the words which man's wisdom teacheth, but which the Holy Ghost teacheth. | Not in words which man's wisdom teacheth, but which the Spirit teacheth. |

This was the reading and translation of the Improved Version.

JOHN xiv. 26.

| *Authorized Version.* | *Revised Version.* |
|---|---|
| But the Comforter, which is the Holy Ghost, whom the Father will send in my name, he shall teach you all things. | But the Comforter,* *even* the Holy Spirit, whom the Father will send in my name, he shall teach you all things.<br><br>[* Or, *Advocate* or *Helper.* |

The 'Spirit of truth' is said in xiv. 16 to be 'another Comforter' to be given to the disciples in answer to the prayer of Jesus. Hence the translation here, the 'Holy Spirit.' The 'Ghost of truth' would have been of course an inadmissible rendering.

----

The Spirit, or Spirit of God, and Holy Spirit of God, are expressions not new to the New Testament writers, and where they occur in the Old Testament the meaning is generally very clear, since, excepting in the few cases in which the reference is to the personal being or mind of God, these terms obviously convey the idea of some divine influence, as power, genius, inspiration. It would have been impossible, therefore, for the Translators of 1611 to use the term 'Ghost' in such cases instead of 'Spirit,' until they came to the New Testament. It was assumed, moreover, that the separate Personality of the Third Subsistence in the Trinity was a special Christian revelation. Nevertheless, by the use of a capital letter in some of the Old Testament instances, as has been observed, this has been, perhaps unconsciously, suggested. The peculiar light of the New Testament, in which the Holy Spirit sometimes appears as if it were a personal Being, was reflected back on certain passages in the older books. The Revisers very properly, as we have seen, alter the form. The following passage is noted here as one which has been supposed to refer specially to the Holy Spirit as the third person of the Divine Trinity:

### Is. xlviii. 16.

| *Authorized Version.* | *Revised Version.* |
| --- | --- |
| And now the Lord God and his Spirit hath sent me. | And now the Lord God hath sent me, and his spirit. |

The Revisers have in this place restored an ambiguity in the original which had disappeared in the Authorized Version. Bishop Lowth quotes a notice of this ambiguity from Origen (contra Cels. i.), with his opinion that the Holy Spirit was to be understood here, not as sending along with the Father, but as sent by him. The new form is in entire harmony with Dr. Noyes' view, who renders 'with his Spirit.' The prophet is appealing to the authority of the inspiration with which he spoke. Mr. S. Sharpe has the same correction in his 'Holy Bible,' 5th ed. of Old Testament, 1883. Those who have imagined that Christ was the person here sent, and that the text contains therefore a plain reference to the Trinity, seem hardly to have sufficiently observed the heresy involved in the idea of the Third Person joining with the First, who by the way is the only one designated by the Divine name, in sending the Second. It will now be seen that such could not have been the meaning of the passage.

---

### General Illustrations.

The following passages illustrate in various ways the improvements of the Revised Version with reference to the question of the Spirit or Holy Spirit of God. The changes will not seem considerable, but they are all more or less important :

### EZEK. xi. 5.

| And the Spirit of the LORD fell upon me, and said unto me, Speak, Thus saith the LORD. | And the spirit of the LORD fell upon me, and he said unto me, Speak, Thus saith the LORD. |
| --- | --- |

### 2 PET. i. 21.

| *Authorized Version.* | *Revised Version.* |
|---|---|
| For the prophecy came not in old time by the will of man; but holy men of God spake as they were moved by the Holy Ghost. | For no prophecy ever came* by the will of man; but men spake from God, being moved by the Holy Ghost.† |
| | [* Or, *was brought.*    † Or, *Holy Spirit.* |

### 2 SAM. xxiii. 2.

| | |
|---|---|
| [David said] The Spirit of the LORD spake by me, and his word was in my tongue. | The spirit of the LORD spake by* me, and his word was upon my tongue.    [* Or, *in.* |

Compare with this last passage the reference to one of the Psalms (cx. 1) in Matt. xxii. 48, 'How then doth David in the Spirit call him Lord?' where the older form, 'in spirit,' though more literal, clearly failed to express the intended idea of an inspired utterance. In the parallel text in Mark (xii. 36), the Revision very properly corrects 'said by the Holy Ghost' to 'said in the Holy Spirit.'

### LUKE ii. 25—27.

| | |
|---|---|
| The Holy Ghost was upon him [Simeon]. And it was revealed unto him by the Holy Ghost, that . . . 27. And he came by the Spirit into the temple. | The Holy Spirit was upon him. And it had been revealed unto him by the Holy Spirit, that . . . 27. And he came in the Spirit into the temple. |

It is clear in this instance that as the Revisers could not say, 'he came by the Ghost into the temple,' they preferred to put Spirit instead of Ghost in the preceding verses.

### JOHN i. 33.

| | |
|---|---|
| Upon whom thou shalt see the Spirit descending, and remaining on him, the same is he which baptizeth with the Holy Ghost. | Upon whomsoever thou shalt see the Spirit descending, and abiding upon him, the same is he that baptizeth with * the Holy Spirit.    [* Or, *in.* |

## Is. lxi. 1.

| *Authorized Version.* | *Revised Version.* |
| --- | --- |
| The Spirit of the Lord God is upon me. | The spirit of the Lord God is upon me. |

In the case of the quotation of this passage by Jesus at Nazareth (Luke iv. 18), the New Testament Company do not follow the rule which the Old Testament Revisers adopt. They leave 'the Spirit of the Lord,' as in the Authorized Version. See Is. xi. 2, 'The spirit of the LORD shall rest upon him, the spirit of wisdom and understanding, the spirit of counsel and might, the spirit of knowledge and of the fear of the LORD.'

## LUKE iv. 1.

| And Jesus being full of the Holy Ghost, returned from Jordan, and was led by the Spirit into the wilderness, being forty days tempted of the devil. | And Jesus full of the Holy Spirit, returned from the Jordan, and was led by* the Spirit in the wilderness during forty days, being tempted of the devil. |
| --- | --- |
| | [* Or, *in.* |

It may be useful to notice here some other passages in which the 'Holy Spirit' is substituted for 'Holy Ghost,' to the manifest advantage of the sense to English readers :

## ACTS vi. 3.

| Seven men of honest report, full of the Holy Ghost and wisdom. | Seven men of good report, full of the Spirit and of wisdom. |
| --- | --- |

The Improved Version bracketed the word 'Holy' as doubtful. It is now omitted, and the Revisers naturally say Spirit, as the second word in Holy Ghost without the first would hardly be considered a reverent term to use. Hence the correction immediately after in—

## ACTS vi. 5.

| *Authorized Version.* | *Revised Version.* |
|---|---|
| They chose Stephen, a man full of faith and of the Holy Ghost. | And they chose Stephen, a man full of faith and of the Holy Spirit. |

## JOHN vii. 39.

| | |
|---|---|
| But this spake he of the Spirit, which they that believe on him should receive : for the Holy Ghost was not yet *given*, because that Jesus was not yet glorified. | But this spake he of the Spirit, which they that believed on him were to receive: for the Spirit* was not yet *given;* because Jesus was not yet glorified.<br><br>[* Some ancient authorities read, *the Holy Spirit.* |

The word 'Holy' was again marked doubtful in the Improved Version. The Revisers omit it, but on that account they were obliged, according to their invariable method when 'Spirit' occurs without the adjective, to translate 'Spirit' instead of 'Ghost.'

## ACTS ii. 4.

| | |
|---|---|
| And they were all filled with the Holy Ghost, and began to speak with other tongues, as the spirit gave them utterance. | And they were all filled with the Holy Spirit, and began to speak with other tongues, as the Spirit gave them utterance. |

The context here has obviously determined the use of 'Spirit' instead of 'Ghost.' The Spirit is given, and the manifestations of the Spirit in wisdom and in various powers are detailed. In the following passage the correction removes an obvious inconsistency in the use of two different terms for the same Spirit.

## 1 COR. xii. 3.

| | |
|---|---|
| That no man speaking by the Spirit of God calleth Jesus accursed : and that no man can say that Jesus is the Lord, but by the Holy Ghost. | That no man speaking in the Spirit of God saith, Jesus is anathema ; and no man can say, Jesus is Lord, but in the Holy Spirit. |

ROM. XV. 30.

| *Authorized Version.* | *Revised Version.* |
|---|---|
| Now I beseech you, brethren, for the Lord Jesus Christ's sake, and for the love of the Spirit, that ye strive together with me in your prayers to God for me. | Now I beseech you, brethren, by our Lord Jesus Christ, and by the love of the Spirit, that ye strive together with me in your prayers to God for me. |

The Improved Version has here the same correction from 'for' to 'by.' The Authorized form had suggested the interpretation of 'the love manifested by the Spirit,' but most modern interpreters translate with the Revisers, and understand the love to be that which the Spirit generates, the chief of the 'fruits of the Spirit.' [Gal. v. 22 ; Philemon 9.] The text is a remarkably clear example of the manner in which Paul distinguished Christ and the Spirit from the God to whom prayer should be made for providential mercies.

There is an obvious improvement in the change in Matt. xxvii. 50, where the Revisers say, instead of 'yielded up the ghost,' 'yielded up his spirit ;' and in John xix. 30, for 'gave up the ghost,' 'gave up his spirit.' But they have retained the old form, 'gave up the ghost,' in Mark xv. 37, and Luke xxiii. 46. In the latter case, the change might almost seem to have been more than suggested by the quotation of Jesus from Ps. xxxi. 5, which Luke specially records, 'Father, into thy hands I commend my spirit.'

The following passage from the Old Testament offers a singular instance of mistranslation. The correction was long since anticipated by Bishop Lowth, Dr. G. V. Smith, Dr. Noyes, and others :

Is. lix. 19.

| When the enemy shall come in like a flood, the Spirit of the LORD shall lift up a standard against him. | For he shall come as a rushing stream, which the breath of the LORD driveth. |

## ON THE DEITY OF CHRIST.

*Some Passages which have been supposed to teach this Doctrine.*

### 1 JOHN iii. 16.

| *Authorized Version.* | *Revised Version.* |
|---|---|
| Hereby perceive we the love *of God*, because he laid down his life for us. | Hereby know we love, because he laid down his life for us. |

Mr. Samuel Sharpe remarks here, 'King James' translators took an unwarrantable liberty' in introducing the word 'God.' Especially, it might be added, in view of Christ's own declaration respecting himself, 'Greater love hath no man than this, that a man 'lay down his life' for his friends' (John xv. 13). But they probably had in their minds the similar expression in chapter iv. 9, in which Christ's coming is described as a manifestation of the love of God. This, again, is parallel with the text in John iii. 16, 'For God so loved the world, that he gave his only begotten Son,' &c. In the present case, however, the word 'he' does not properly represent to the English reader the force of the Greek pronoun, which refers back to the prior antecedent in verse 8, viz. the Son of God who was 'manifested that he might destroy the works of the devil.'

---

### ACTS xx. 28.

| To feed the church of God, which he hath purchased with his own blood. | To feed the church of God,* which he purchased† with his own blood. |
|---|---|
| | [* Many ancient authorities read *the Lord.*  † Gr. *acquired.* |

Compare with this, ' Even as Christ also loved the church, and gave himself up for it' (Eph. v. 25, R.V.). 'The churches of Christ' occurs once (Rom. xvi. 16), and he says, in Matt. xvi. 18, ' Upon this rock I will build my church.' But in some five or six other places the phrase is, ' the church (or churches) of God.' Nevertheless, the expression ' blood of God' appears in no other place in the Bible; and when the phrase came to be employed by ecclesiastical writers, it was rejected, it is said, by Athanasius, with horror, as an invention of the Arians, who, regarding Christ as a subordinate God, could without difficulty employ the words in relation to him. The American Revisers urge that the text should read, ' the church of the Lord,' with a note simply stating that ' some ancient authorities, including the two oldest MSS., read, ' God.'' The state of opinion at the time when these copies were made had probably something to do with this various reading.

---

### 1 TIM. iii. 16.

*Authorized Version.*

And without controversy great is the mystery of godliness: God was manifest in the flesh, justified in the Spirit, seen of angels, preached unto the Gentiles, believed on in the world, received up into glory.

*Revised Version.*

And without controversy great is the mystery of godliness; He who* was manifested in the flesh, justified in the Spirit, seen of angels, preached among the nations, believed on in the world, received up in glory.

[* The word *God* in place of *He who* rests on no sufficient ancient evidence. Some ancient authorities read, *which*.

This was also the reading and the translation of the Improved Version. 'The mystery of godliness is great: He who was manifested in the flesh was justified by the

Spirit,' &c.  The sense would have been clearer if the tense-form, 'was justified,' had been expressed in the Revised Version, so completing the sentence as it really stands in the original.[1]  Mr. Sharpe says, 'This important change in meaning depends upon a single letter in the Greek; and in the celebrated manuscript in the British Museum, called the Alexandrian Manuscript, some dishonest reader has endeavoured to change the 'One who' into 'God,' by altering the letter.  But fortunately the attempt is betrayed and defeated by the difference in colour between the ancient and the modern ink.'  This was the second of the corruptions (the other being the text of the Three Witnesses in 1 John v. 7, now removed from the Bible as spurious) on which Sir Isaac Newton wrote in his work on 'Two Notable Corruptions of Scripture.'  Dean Alford, observing how completely the sentence was marred and disjoined by the substitution of the word God, so strenuously upheld even to this day by some, adds: 'There is hardly a passage in the New Testament in which I feel more deep personal thankfulness for the restoration of the true and wonderful connection of the original.'  Yet no text in the Bible has been more often or more urgently appealed to in support of the Trinitarian dogma of the Deity of Christ.

In this place may be cited a passage in which the words God and Christ stand so closely together in the New Version, that some might possibly mistake the meaning of the writer, as though he intended to say 'God, that is, Christ.'  It illustrates also further 'the mystery' of the citation just given:

---

[1] It was so translated by Mr. Edgar Taylor, a Unitarian layman, in his 'New Testament of our Lord and Saviour Jesus Christ, revised from the Authorized Version, with the aid of other Translations, and made conformable to the Greek Text of J. J. Griesbach, 1839'—'He who was manifested in the flesh, was justified in the Spirit,' &c.

## COL. ii. 2, 3.

| *Authorized Version.* | *Revised Version.* |
|---|---|
| To the acknowledgment of the mystery of God, and of the Father, and of Christ, in whom are hid all the treasures of wisdom and knowledge. | That they may know the mystery of God, *even\** Christ, in whom are all the treasures of wisdom and knowledge hidden. |
| | [\* The ancient authorities vary much in the text of this passage. |

Dean Alford's remarks on this passage are most instructive. 'It is almost impossible to say what was the original reading.' 'The additions here found in the Received Text, and in other authorities, seem to be owing to the common practice in the MSS. of annotating in the margin on the Divine name, to specify to which Person it belonged. Thus it would seem likely that 'of God' having been all that was in the original, 'the Father' was placed against it by some, 'Christ' or 'the Christ' by others; and then these found their way into the text in various combinations, some of which from their difficulty gave rise again to alterations.' He reads and translates, 'the mystery of God, wherein are all the hidden treasures of wisdom and knowledge;' adding, nevertheless, that the mystery was in fact Christ, as shown in chap. i. 27.

---

## ROM. ix. 5.

| | |
|---|---|
| Whose are the fathers, and of whom as concerning the flesh Chris· *came*, who is over all, God blessed for ever. Amen. | Whose are the fathers, and of whom is Christ as concerning the flesh,\* who is over all, God blessed for ever. Amen. |
| | [\* Some modern interpreters place a full stop after *flesh*, and translate, *He who is God over all be (is) blessed for ever;* or, *He who is over all is God blessed for ever.* Others punctuate, *flesh, who is over all. God be (is) blessed for ever.* |

Although the Revisers adhere to the common punctuation and translation of this verse, they indicate in the note how completely the sense depends on the punctuation adopted, there being no stops in the original MS.  The American Revisers would have substituted for this marginal note only one of these variations, thus : 'Or, *flesh : he who is over all, God, be blessed for ever.*'  In the Improved Version, the passage reads, 'God who is over all be blessed for ever.' Mr. Samuel Sharpe translated, in his 'Holy Bible,' 'Of whom was the Christ according to the flesh.  He that is God over all [be] blessed for ever;' remarking in a note elsewhere that the word 'blessed' is never in the New Testament applied otherwise than to the Almighty.'  He has also pointed to the following passage as indicating Paul's manner of thought and expression on the subject in question :

2 COR. xi. 31.

| *Authorized Version.* | *Revised Version.* |
|---|---|
| The God and Father of our Lord Jesus Christ, which is blessed for evermore, knoweth that I lie not. | The God and Father of the Lord Jesus, he who is blessed for evermore,* knoweth, &c. [* Gr. *unto the ages.* |

The parallel is the more striking, inasmuch as the Greek which the Revisers translate here 'He who,' is the same which Paul uses in the text above cited.  It will be remarked that the subjoined 'Amen' in that passage suggests that it should be interpreted as a doxology, and not, as in the Authorized Version, a bare theological statement.

REV. i. 10, 11.

| | |
|---|---|
| I heard behind me a great voice, as of a trumpet, saying, I am Alpha and Omega, the first and the last, and what thou seest write in a book. | I heard behind me a great voice, as of a trumpet, saying, What thou seest write in a book. |

The excision here of the peculiar title which in i. 8 is given expressly to the Lord God the Almighty (as also to God, xxi. 6), is noteworthy, although it partly appears in the speech of the 'one like unto a Son of Man' (i. 17). 'Fear not, I am the first and the last, and the Living One ; and I was dead, and behold I am alive for evermore.' In chapter xxii. 13, where it again occurs in full, 'I am the Alpha and the Omega, the first and the last, the beginning and the end,' the utterer of the words is not clearly indicated. In Isaiah (xli. 4 and xliv. 6) the idea is introduced, not as a definition of the Deity, but as a ground of assurance that his word of prophecy should not fail. Mr. Sharpe says, 'The words, 'I am Alpha and Omega, the first and the last,' added (in i. 11), without sufficient authority, in the Authorized Version, are very important, because in verse 8 they had been spoken by God, and here they are put into the speech of Jesus, thus making him use a title for himself which seems to belong only to the Father.' The Revised Version omits the words in this place, as the Improved Version had done, after the example of Newcome and with the authority of Griesbach. An argument may still be made from their appearance in chap. xxii., and from the partial use of them in chap. i. 17, but in the present clear case it is decided that they form no part of the words attributed to Jesus.

---

### Eph. iii. 9.

| *Authorized Version.* | *Revised Version.* |
|---|---|
| ... In God, who created all things by Jesus Christ. | ... In God, who created all things. |

The additional words in the Authorized Version are now omitted as an interpolation, perhaps a marginal note copied into the text. There is no such idea as that of the creation of the physical world by Jesus Christ even suggested in the Revised Version. The Revisers allow the spurious addition to drop out of the Bible without any marginal notice, as was done also in the case of the notorious text of the Three Witnesses. The Improved Version omitted the words, but not without giving good reasons for the rejection of this interpolation.

What the Authorized translators supposed to have been in the writer's mind appears rather in the corresponding Epistle to the Colossians, which does speak of a creation through Christ. Calvin, with others, understood the word there to describe the moral and spiritual 'renovation included in the benefit of redemption,' the new creation foretold in Isaiah lxv. 17 ('For behold I create new heavens, and a new earth'), and further illustrated by Paul almost in the very strain of the prophet, 'If any man is in Christ *he* is a new creature,' or, says the Revised margin, '*there is* a new creation,' 2 Cor. v. 17.

---

COL. i. 15—18.

| *Authorized Version.* | *Revised Version.* |
|---|---|
| Who is the image of the invisible God, the firstborn of every creature.[1]  For by him were all things created that are in heaven and that are in earth, visible and invisible, whether they be thrones or dominions or principalities or powers: all things were created by him, and for him: and he is before | Who is the image of the invisible God, the firstborn of all creation ; for in him were all things created in the heavens and upon the earth, things visible and things invisible, whether thrones or dominions or principalities or powers ; all things have been created through him, and unto him ; |

---

[1] The Revisers make the same correction in Col. i. 23: 'The gospel which ye have heard, and which was preached to every creature which is under heaven,' now reads, 'The gospel which ye heard, which was preached in all creation under heaven,' that is, to the people of all nations, showing that it was the moral, not the physical, universe that was in the mind of the writer.

| *Authorized Version.* | *Revised Version.* |
|---|---|
| all things, and by him all things consist. And he is the head of the body, the church: who is the beginning, the firstborn from the dead, that in all things he might have the preeminence. | and he is before all things, and in him all things consist.* And he is the head of the body, the church; who is the beginning, the firstborn from the dead, that† in all things he might have the preeminence. |

[* That is, *hold together*. † Or, *that among all he might have.*

Slight as the changes in this important passage may seem, they materially alter the whole tenour of it. Creation in Christ, and in him all things being centred or held together, suggest ideas very different from those conveyed by the Authorized Version. So in John i. 2, where it is said, 'all things were made by' the Logos, the margin adds, 'or, *through*,' and it has the same note to *v.* 10, 'The world was made by ('or, *through*') him, and the world knew him not.' Compare the kindred forms of thought in the late Epistle in which God is said to have spoken now by *his* Son, who is—

### HEB. i. 3.

| . . . . the brightness of his glory, and the express image of his person. | . . . . the effulgence of his glory, and the* very image of his substance.[1] |

[* Or, *the impress of his substance.*

And on whose 'preeminence in every respect' the writer

[1] It is remarked by Mr. Gordon that 'as regards the question which formed the kernel of the historic controversy between the followers of St. Athanasius and the successors of Arius, whether our Lord is 'of the same substance' or 'of like substance' with the Father, the Revision unexpectedly leans to the Homoiousian, that is, to the Arian side. . . . The Revisers allot the first place, giving thus the sign of their deliberate approval, as Scriptural, to language which accords neither with the Nicæan Creed, nor with the 39 Articles, nor with the Westminster Confession.'—*Christian Doctrine in the Light of New Testament Revision*, by Alexander Gordon, M.A., 1882.

proceeds to dilate throughout the Epistle. He had just contrasted the partial revelations from God by prophets with this now given—

HEB. i. 2.

| *Authorized Version.* | *Revised Version.* |
|---|---|
| ... by his Son whom he hath appointed heir of all things, by whom also he made the worlds. | ... in his Son* whom he appointed heir of all things, through whom also he made the worlds.† |
|  | [* Gr. *a Son*.    † Gr. *ages*. |

It appears very plainly in the New Version that the writers of these passages had in view the dispensation of the fulness of the times (Eph. i. 10), the new constitution of things, the new creation in the spiritual world that was now accomplished in Christ, but which had been in the mind of God from the beginning. So the author of the Epistle to the Colossians says, in applying this to the members of the body of which Christ is the head, 'Ye have put on the new man which is being renewed unto knowledge after the image of him that created him' (R.V.); and to the Ephesians (iv. 24), 'and put on the new man which after God hath been created in righteousness and holiness of truth' (R.V.). And again, 'For we are his workmanship, created in Christ Jesus for good works, which God afore prepared that we should walk in them' (R.V.).

That the margin gives here the true translation seems probable from the fact that the Scriptures, in common with other ancient writings, speak of but one material world. The plural, 'worlds,' occurs in the Authorized Version in only one other place, and that in the present Epistle; and there also, as the Revised margin indicates, the Greek has the same term as here (Heb. xi. 3, marg. 'Gr. *ages*'). In the Revised Version appears the expression, 'before the worlds' in 1 Cor. ii. 7 (marg. 'or, *ages*'). In the passage in He-brews just adverted to, it is not clear why the writer should have introduced his long record of the saints who had been accepted for their faith in the things 'not seen as yet,' by an assertion of the doctrine of material creation out of nothing ; and it is by no means certain that he meant the starry worlds, to use a modern phrase, and not the framing of the ages or dispensations in the sense above explained (see p. 62).

In the present instance the natural sense of the word, as given in the margin, harmonizes with the entire purport of the Epistle, which was to show that in Christ the ancient promises and foreshadowings were realized. He was the appointed heir of all the ages.

The attribution of very lofty prerogatives to Christ in the New Testament, especially in the Pauline writings, has never been doubted by Unitarian scholars. They only affirm that these are uniformly represented there as the gift of the Father to him. Their relative positions are clearly indicated in another writing, in a passage which also throws further light upon the expressions in Heb. i. 2. At the text in Eph. iii. 11, 'According to the eternal purpose, which he purposed in Christ Jesus our Lord,' the Revised margin says, 'or, *purpose of the ages*,' a phrase without clear mean-ing in itself, but which probably indicates the direction of the true sense, if it be remembered that the word preceding 'the ages' does not primarily mean 'purpose,' but a 'setting forth, pre-arranging, or disposing.' The idea would there-fore be, 'According to the determining or pre-arrangement of the ages in the Divine order.'

It will be noticed in the Revised context of the passage just cited that the wisdom of the Divine purpose was to be made known 'through the church,' not 'known by the church,' as in the Old Version (Eph. iii. 10) ; a marked improvement.

F

### HEB. iii. 5, 6.

| *Authorized Version.* | *Revised Version.* |
|---|---|
| And Moses verily was faithful in all his house as a servant. . . . But Christ as a Son over his own house. | And Moses indeed was faithful in all his* house as a servant. . . . but Christ as a son over his* house. |
| | [* That is, *God's house.* See Num. xii. 7. |

The Improved Version translated here, 'in all the household *of God*,' which gave indeed a correct paraphrase, but not an accurate rendering, as was in fact acknowledged in the subjoined note (Gr. '*in all his household*'). The passage referred to in the Revised margin reads, ' My servant Moses is not so, who is faithful in all mine house.' The interpretation thus furnished, while enabling the reader to see his way through the ambiguities of the possessive pronoun in this sentence, gives at the same time a clear reply to the suggestion that the writer intended to identify the Son over God's house with God himself just before referred to.

---

### PHIL. ii. 6, 7.

| | |
|---|---|
| Who, being in the form of God, thought it not robbery to be equal with God, but made himself of no reputation, and took upon him the form of a servant, and was made in the likeness of men. | Who, being* in the form of God, counted it not a prize† to be on an equality with God, but emptied himself, taking the form of a servant,‡ being made§ in the likeness of men. |
| | [* Gr. *being originally.*  † Gr. *a thing to be grasped at.*  ‡ Gr. *bondservant.*  § Gr. *becoming in.* |

The Improved Version anticipated the chief correction in this passage, thus, 'did not esteem as a prey this resemblance to God, but divested himself of it' (note, ' Gr. *emptied him-*

*self'*). The Revisers say in their margin, that instead of 'a prize,' the Greek may be translated, 'a thing to be grasped at.' The American Revision Company urge that this should have been the translation in the text. They say, Let the text run, 'counted not the being on an equality with God a thing to be grasped.' Dean Alford says, 'to grasp at.' What the author meant by the being like God, which Jesus forbore to claim until the time appointed of the Father, in the spirit of benevolent self-abnegation for which his example is here commended to the Philippian brethren, may be understood from what is said of him in his glorified state in other passages of this Epistle; as, for example, in iii. 21, where is ascribed to him the ability 'to subject all things unto himself.' See 1 Cor. xv. 25, also Ps. cx. 1, the original source of these Messianic conceptions. Compare also what the writer says here, in verse 9, of the high exaltation to which God raised Jesus in reward for his self-sacrificing humility, that all should confess that he 'is Lord, to the glory of God the Father.' But exaltation surely means raising to a higher state of glory. Christ has become what he was not before; so that the 'being originally' in the form of God which the margin suggests, gives little help to the interpretation and is not necessary, the original word as found in other places conveying no such idea. The terms used in verse 6 to describe what Jesus really was, and of course knew himself to be, must be understood in view of the fact of this subsequent exaltation. They cannot mean more than is described in verse 9. The Revised Version gives at least a view more in harmony with the doctrine of Heb. xii. 2, that Jesus, 'for the joy that was set before him endured the cross, despising shame, and hath sat down at the right hand of the throne of God,' than was presented in the Authorized Version in the phrase, 'thought it not robbery to be equal with God,' which has been often quoted as implying that he was therefore God's equal; that is to say, himself God.

PHIL. ii. 9—11.

| Authorized Version. | Revised Version. |
|---|---|
| Wherefore God also hath highly exalted him, and given him a name which is above every name: that at the name of Jesus every knee should bow, of *things* in heaven, and *things* in earth, and *things* under the earth, and that every tongue should confess that Jesus Christ is Lord, to the glory of God the Father. | Wherefore also God highly exalted him, and gave unto him the name which is above every name; that in the name of Jesus every knee should bow, of *things* in heaven, and *things* on earth, and *things* under the earth,* and that every tongue should confess that Jesus Christ is Lord, to the glory of God the Father. |
|  | [* Or, *things of the world below.* |

So the Improved Version, 'in the name of Jesus.' Mr. S. Sharpe says of this more correct translation, 'The meaning is that every man should worship the Almighty as a Christian, owning himself a disciple of Jesus, which is worshipping in his name.' 'From the mistranslation of this passage,' he adds, 'has arisen the reverent but unauthorized custom of bowing in church whenever the word 'Jesus' is mentioned.'[1]

MATT. xxviii. 18.

| | |
|---|---|
| All power is given unto me in heaven and in earth. | All authority hath been given unto me in heaven and on earth. |

JOHN xvii. 2.

| | |
|---|---|
| As thou hast given him power over all flesh. | Even as thou gavest him authority over all flesh. |

In both these passages the Revisers have gone beyond the Improved Version, which retained the Authorized 'power.' In Matt. x. 1, where the Authorized Version says that Jesus gave his disciples 'power against unclean spirits,' they correct

---

[1] This practice, which was first adopted at the recitation of the 'Credo,' is not uncommonly now followed, as Mr. Sharpe says, whenever in the course of the prayers the name of Jesus occurs.

to 'authority over,' the original word being the same as in the two texts just given. But this word is used also in Matt. ix. 6, 8, which should therefore have been, 'that the Son of Man hath authority on earth to forgive sins,' and the multitude 'glorified God, which had given such authority unto men.'[1] They say, however, in the margin against the word power, ' or, *authority*.' The like correction in the passage following is important, and in this instance the Improved Version has the same: not 'the power,' but 'the authority':

REV. xii. 10.

| *Authorized Version.* | *Revised Version.* |
|---|---|
| And I heard a loud voice saying in heaven, Now is come salvation, and strength, and the kingdom of our God, and the power of his Christ. | And I heard a great voice in heaven, saying, Now* is come the salvation, and the power, and the kingdom of our God, and the authority of his Christ. |
| | [* Or, *now is the salvation, &c., become our God's, and the authority is become his Christ's.* |

ROM. xiv. 10.

| | |
|---|---|
| We shall all stand before the judgment-seat of Christ. | For we shall all stand before the judgment-seat of God. |

This correction in the reading is specially noteworthy from the quotation which immediately follows: ' For it is written, As I live, saith the Lord, to me every knee shall bow, and every tongue shall confess to God' (Is. xlv. 23); on which Paul adds, 'so then each one of us shall give account of himself to God.' It is true that elsewhere (2 Cor. v. 10) the same writer affirms that 'We must all be made

---

[1] This is one of the amendments which was urged without effect by the American Company of Revisers, and which they considered of sufficient importance to be placed on record. They say, 'Matt. ix. 6, 8, Mark ii. 10, and Luke v. 24, for 'power' to forgive sins, read 'authority,' as is now indicated in the margin, and as the word is elsewhere translated.'

manifest before the judgment-seat of Christ,' having just before said, ' We make it our aim to be well-pleasing unto him.' But in the verses following the Authorized text above, which is now amended, there was an obvious identification of Christ with the Jehovah of the prophet.

As to the meaning of the passage in 2 Cor. v. 10, it is sufficient to remark that it corresponds with Paul's representation in Rom. ii. 16, ' In the day when God shall judge the secrets of men, according to my gospel, by Jesus Christ.' The same idea is presented in his reported speech at Athens (Acts xvii. 31), ' Inasmuch as he hath appointed a day in the which he will judge the world in righteousness by (marg. ' or, *in*') the man (marg. ' or, *a man*') whom he hath ordained ;' this highest function being thus attributed to a human being, one who could be properly called a man, with no hint of his being at the same time anything else, which was indeed the point of the Apostle's statement.

The almost omniscience, however, which this grand function would seem to attribute to Christ, is not attested, as has been supposed, by the statement in John ii. 24, 25, where the Revised margin suggests the following : ' He needed not that any one should bear witness concerning a man, for he himself knew what was in the man.'

---

### JOHN x. 14, 15.

| *Authorized Version.* | *Revised Version.* |
|---|---|
| I am the good shepherd, and know my sheep, and am known of mine. As the Father knoweth me, even so know I the Father. | I am the good shepherd ; and I know mine own, and mine own know me, even as the Father knoweth me, and I know the Father. |

An amendment partially anticipated in the Improved Version, and altogether in the latter portion, which had been supposed to indicate some mystic communion of mutual intimacy between the Father and the Son.

There are two passages in which the Revisers have altogether changed the sense of the Authorized Version in favour of the orthodox belief that Christ is God.

## 2 PET. i. 1, 2.

*Authorized Version.*

To them that have obtained like precious faith with us through the righteousness of God, and our Saviour Jesus Christ, grace and peace be multiplied unto you through the knowledge of God and of Jesus our Lord.

*Revised Version.*

To them that have obtained a like precious faith with us in the righteousness of our God* and Saviour Jesus Christ : grace to you and peace be multiplied in the knowledge of God and of Jesus our Lord.

[* Or, *our God, and the Saviour.*

## TIT. ii. 13.

Looking for that blessed hope and the glorious appearing of the great God, and our Saviour Jesus Christ.

Looking for the blessed hope and appearing of the glory of our great God* and Saviour Jesus Christ.

[* Or, *of the great God, and our Saviour.*

In both cases, it is a simple matter of translation ; there is no question about the text. It is acknowledged in the notes that two distinct beings may be referred to, and the immediate context, in at least the first instance, shows that two beings were intended, since the knowledge 'of Jesus our Lord' is plainly distinguished from 'the knowledge of God.'

With regard to the second passage, Dean Alford comes to the same conclusion, after carefully considering the other instances in the Pastoral Epistles in which God and Christ are named together in such a manner as to preclude the possibility of identifying them as one. The Authorized rendering is, he says, 'both structurally and contextually more probable, and more agreeable to the Apostle's way of writing.'[1] The American Revisers also adopt this view. They

---

[1] 'The New Testament for English Readers,' by Henry Alford, D.D., Dean of Canterbury, 1865.

say with reference to both passages, ' Let the text and margin
exchange places.' They do not agree with the English New
Testament Company that the alteration in the text in these
two passages is an improvement, or believe that the writers
certainly mean to say that Jesus was our God, or our great
God.

In the second text the revision offers one marked improvement. It is no longer 'the appearing of God,' which is not
a Scriptural phrase or idea, but of 'the glory' of God, which
is. See Matt. xvi. 27, and Mark viii. 38. In the Authorized
Version, the last clause appears ambiguous from the omission,
as in the other text, of the word 'of.' The same ambiguity
is found in another passage which the Revisers have not
altered, 'According to the grace of our God, and the Lord
Jesus Christ' (2 Thes. i. 12).

In this passage the Greek construction is exactly the same
as in the two cases quoted above, as has been remarked by
Dr. G. Vance Smith,[1] who, however, thinks that the Revised
rendering may possibly be the correct one, at least in the
passage from 2 Peter, that Epistle having been one of the
latest writings of the New Testament, and belonging to a
period when Christ was spoken of personally as God. But
the distinction is clearly marked in other parts of the Epistle
to Titus between God our Saviour and Christ our Saviour,
as it is also in Jude 25, 'To the only God our Saviour,
through Jesus Christ our Lord' (R.V.).

----

A few other changes may be suitably mentioned here, in
which the Revision might seem at first glance to incline in
the same direction as the revisions just cited. But they are
readings, not renderings, and they present no real difficulty
to Unitarian scholars. For example, in Acts xvi. 7: 'But
the Spirit suffered them not' occurs in the Authorized Version after the statement that Paul and Silas 'were forbidden

----

[1] 'Texts and Margins,' p. 42.

of the Holy Ghost to preach the word in Asia.' The Revised Version reads, ' the Spirit of Jesus suffered them not,' according to all the three oldest MSS., so clearly identifying the Holy Spirit with the Spirit of Jesus. There is nothing in this expression contrary to Unitarian views, whether as to the Supreme God, or the powers conferred by him upon Christ, however difficult it may be to harmonize such a statement with the orthodox standards.

---

### PHIL. iv. 13.

| *Authorized Version.* | *Revised Version.* |
|---|---|
| I can do all things through Christ that strengtheneth me. | I can do all things in him that strengtheneth me. |

Meaning, probably, Christ (see 1 Tim. i. 12 ; 2 Cor. xii. 9), but the word is omitted as a gloss, not being found, says Alford, in the oldest MSS. The Improved Version made the same omission. On the other hand, it anticipated the Revised change in Philemon 20, refresh my heart ' in Christ' from ' in the Lord' of the Authorized ; and also the correction now made in—

### EPH. v. 29.

Even as the Lord the church. | Even as Christ also the church.

---

In a few other passages the Revisers exchange 'God' or 'the Lord' for Christ, but without detriment to Unitarian interpretation. For example, in Rom. x. 17, 'and hearing by the word of God,' now reads, 'and hearing by the word of Christ.' (See p. 97.)

### COL. iii. 15.

| And let the peace of God rule in your hearts. | And let the peace of Christ rule* in your hearts. |
|---|---|
| | [* Gr. *arbitrate*. |

This is the reading of the Improved Version.

1 PET. iii. 15.

| *Authorized Version.* | *Revised Version.* |
| --- | --- |
| But sanctify the Lord God in your hearts. | But sanctify in your hearts Christ as Lord. |

ROM. xiv. 4.

| For God is able to make him stand. | For the Lord hath power to make him stand. |
| --- | --- |

Judging from the context, this may be the true reading, and by 'the Lord' the Apostle may have meant the glorified Son of God. 'God hath power' would read almost like a truism. There is, however, a passage from another writer in which the Revision changes 'God' to 'Lord,' and obviously without altering the sense. In James iii. 9, instead of 'therewith bless we God, even the Father,' we now read, 'the Lord and Father.'

It is proper to remark in this connection that on the text, 'The only begotten Son which is in the bosom of the Father,' John i. 18, occurs the note, 'Many ancient authorities read, *God only begotten*'—a kind of expression quite familiar with Arius and his followers. Strictly speaking, it should be, 'an only-begotten God,' and, having no definite article, the phrase would correspond with the use of the word 'God' in its secondary sense in the last clause of John i. 1.

---

JUDE 4.

| Denying the only Lord God, and our Lord Jesus Christ. | Denying our only Master* and Lord Jesus Christ. [ *Or, *the only Master, and our Lord Jesus Christ.* |
| --- | --- |

The Revisers have followed Griesbach in omitting 'God,' and it may be supposed that it was a gloss which found its way afterwards into the text. Perhaps the strongest point in favour of this reading is that the same word is used in the corresponding passage in 2 Pet. ii. 1, 'denying even the Master that bought them,' as the New Version translates.

### The Worship of Christ.

Among the arguments in favour of the Deity of Christ,
one of the most popular is the fact that he is said to have
been 'worshipped' by various persons in his lifetime on
earth.   This worship is conceived to have begun with the
homage paid to him in his infancy by the wise men (marg.
'Gr. *Magi*') from the East (Matt. ii. 2, 11, see also verse 8).
But at this very chapter the American Revisers recommend
the addition of a very important note, to the effect that 'the
Greek word denotes an act of reverence, whether paid to
man, see Matt. xviii. 26 ('The servant therefore fell down
and worshipped him,' viz. 'a certain king'), or to God,
Matt. iv. 10 ('Thou shalt worship the Lord thy God').'

In the passages (about a dozen) in the Gospels in which
it is said that persons came to Jesus and worshipped him,
the contexts sufficiently show that the word must be understood in the sense of 'paying homage,' not of religious
adoration, the same sense in which Cornelius is stated to
have worshipped Peter (Acts x. 25).   Only in one place do
the circumstances appear to favour the other use of the word
in reference to Christ, viz. in Luke xxiv. 52: 'And it came
to pass while he blessed them, he was parted from them,
and carried up into heaven.   And they worshipped him, and
returned to Jerusalem with great joy, and were continually
in the temple, blessing God'—in the Authorized Version,
'praising and blessing God.'   The distinction is thus observed
between the two kinds of reverence, but also the notes in
the margin should be remarked: (1) 'Some ancient authorities omit *was carried up into heaven.*'   (2) 'Some ancient
authorities omit *worshipped him, and.*'

The Revisers have changed the word 'worship' used in
Luke xiv. 10, in the Authorized Version, in the old English
sense of respect paid to any one, which obtains in most of

the passages above referred to, into 'glory,' which the Greek word in this instance properly means.

---

### LUKE xxiii. 42.

*Authorized Version.*

And he said unto Jesus, Lord, remember me when thou comest into thy kingdom.

*Revised Version.*

And he said, Jesus, remember me when thou comest in thy kingdom.*

[* Some ancient authorities read, *into thy kingdom.*

This has been often described as an act of worship, an idea not necessarily suggested even in the Authorized Version. In the Revised form the act appears quite simple and natural, especially if the speaker believed, with the early disciples generally, that Jesus was to come again 'in his kingdom.' 'Coming into thy kingdom' conveys a different idea.

---

### ACTS vii. 59.

And they stoned Stephen, calling *upon God*, and saying, Lord Jesus, receive my spirit.

And they stoned Stephen, calling upon *the Lord*, and saying, Lord Jesus, receive my spirit.

In the Improved Version the phrase is 'invoking and saying,' which is substantially all that the original justifies. Perhaps a more familiar modern term would be, 'appealing for help and saying.' In any case the word used does not necessarily mean praying to God; and that the Revision inserts the right person, if any need be named, may be argued from the fact that the martyr saw Jesus in a vision, standing, as he said, 'on the right hand of God,' distinguishing therefore plainly between them, and in effect appealing, not to God who was invisible, but to him whom he saw thus standing in the place of honour near him. 'At the right hand of God' could only mean in a state of highest exaltation.

---

## COL. iii. 16.

| *Authorized Version.* | *Revised Version.* |
|---|---|
| Let the word of Christ dwell in you richly in all wisdom, teaching and admonishing one another in psalms and hymns and spiritual songs, singing with grace in your hearts to the Lord. | Let the word of Christ * dwell in you richly in all wisdom; teaching and admonishing one another † with psalms and hymns and spiritual songs, singing with grace in your hearts unto God. |

[* Some ancient authorities read, *the Lord*, others *God*.          † Or, *yourselves.*

The Improved Version had the important correction in this place, which shows God to be the single Object of worship, so bringing the text into harmony with the following verse.    Dean Alford admits this, observing that it has the authority of 'all our oldest MSS.'

---

## JOHN xvi. 23, 24, 26.

| | |
|---|---|
| And in that day ye shall ask me nothing: Verily, verily, I say unto you, whatsoever ye shall ask the Father in my Name, he will give it you. Hitherto have ye asked nothing in my Name: ask, and ye shall receive. | And in that day ye shall ask * me nothing. Verily, verily, I say unto you, If ye shall ask anything of the Father, he will give it you in my name.    Hitherto have ye asked nothing in my name: ask, and ye shall receive. |
| 26. At that day, ye shall ask in my Name: and I say not unto you that I will pray the Father for you; for the Father himself loveth you. | 26. In that day ye shall ask in my name: and I say not unto you, that I will pray † the Father for you; for the Father himself loveth you. |

[* Or, *ask me no questions*.   † Gr. *make request of.*

The sanction for the practice of praying through, or in the name of, Jesus Christ, is usually found in these texts.

It should be noted, therefore, (1) that in *v.* 23, where the expression occurs of asking in Christ's name, we now have also gifts from God in his name, gifts of the kind which may perhaps be sufficiently understood from the prayer of the Apostles in Acts iv. 30, 'that signs and wonders may be done through the name of thy holy Servant Jesus' (R.V.), and Acts iii. 6, (2) that asking in Christ's name may thus be understood to mean on behalf of Christ's cause.    There is nothing here to show that prayer, in order to be effectual, must be offered in the name of Christ.

In this view of the meaning of the phrase may perhaps be explained an addition made in John xiv. 14, which now reads, 'If ye shall ask me anything in my name.' It is, indeed, noted in the margin that 'many ancient authorities omit *me*,' but the reading is admitted in the text, and the question will naturally suggest itself, what can be meant by asking Christ in his own name, unless it be for help in the carrying on of his work.[1]

---

[1] This interpretation of the phrase is confirmed by reference to the preceding context of this passage (*vv.* 12, 13), which Campbell translates, 'He who believeth on me shall himself do such works as I do; nay, even greater than these shall he do; because I go to my Father, and will do whatsoever ye shall ask in my name.' See, for example, Acts iii. 6: 'In the name of Jesus Christ of Nazareth, walk' (R.V.).

# SUPPOSED ALLUSIONS TO CHRIST IN THE OLD TESTAMENT.

For lessons of specifically Christian doctrine, we naturally look to the New Testament : the amendments in the Revised Version which bear upon points of evangelical theology will be found there in abundance.

But the Church teaches that at least the rudiments of the gospel may be discovered in the Old Testament also, and thus that the light of Christian times is thrown back upon the earlier revelations of Divine truth.

It is especially insisted upon that, though only in some confused way, the Christ of the New Testament was the Jehovah of the Old, and it materially favours this identification that the term ' LORD' is employed in the Old Testament to stand for the proper name Jehovah, while the same word is used with some ambiguity by the New Testament writers.

It is also believed by orthodox theologians that the older Scriptures foretold everything of importance in relation to the life and work, the death and resurrection of Christ, both as to the facts and their interpretation.  The Jewish people held the doctrine of Messianic prophecy, and it was from them that the Christians learned it, and applied it in their own way to their Master.

Now in both cases the orthodox views depend on infer-ence, and a large amount of believing ingenuity is required to make out clearly the relation between type and antitype, prediction and fulfilment.  The question has little to do with correct renderings of Old Testament passages.  It is a matter of preconception, not of logical proof.

But even upon these points some fresh light is thrown by
the Revision in certain of what have been called proof-texts
for New Testament doctrine implied or foreshadowed, and
in a few cases, as is supposed, plainly set forth in the Old.
The following are the passages chiefly relied upon—

### GEN. iii. 15.

| *Authorized Version.* | *Revised Version.* |
|---|---|
| And I will put enmity be-tween thee and the woman, and between thy seed and her seed; it shall bruise thy head, and thou shalt bruise his heel. | And I will put enmity be-tween thee and the woman, and between thy seed and her seed; it shall bruise* thy head, and thou shalt bruise* his heel. |
| | [* Or, *lie in wait for.* |

The Revisers' alternative translation for 'bruise,' 'or, *lie
in wait for,*' corresponds with Mr. Wellbeloved's note, ' or,
watch to hurt,' expressions which show more clearly that
the thing indicated was the mutual repulsion and hostility
between the serpent tribe and mankind. They leave, however, ' his heel,' probably by inadvertence. It should be ' its,'
to correspond with the ' it' just before. The Authorized word
' his,' which formerly had this meaning, has certainly appeared
to modern readers to favour the common view, that this was
the first prediction of the Saviour's temporary defeat on Cal-
vary and subsequent conquest over the devil. The Quarterly
Reviewer[1] says, it is well known that " this verse is the earliest
foreshadowing of the hope of the Gospel. . . . but according to
the Revisers, the sinful, sorrowing pair (Adam and Eve) were
to be comforted by the thought that a mutual ' lying in wait'
should always be going on between the human race and the
serpent species." But there is no idea of comforting in the
story, and not a word said to imply that the spirit of Evil
was in the serpent. The account reads quite naturally as it
stands, especially with the marginal explanation.

---

[1] 'Quarterly Review,' October, 1885.

## GEN. xlix. 10.

| *Authorized Version.* | *Revised Version.* |
|---|---|
| The sceptre shall not depart from Judah, nor a lawgiver from between his feet, until Shiloh come, and unto him shall the gathering of the people be. | The sceptre shall not depart from Judah, nor the ruler's staff* from between his feet, until Shiloh come,† and unto him shall the obedience of the peoples be. |

[* Or, *a lawgiver.*   † Or, *till he come to Shiloh, having the obedience of the peoples;* or, as read by the Septuagint, *until that which is his shall come.* Another ancient rendering is, *till he come whose it is,* &c.

In this difficult passage Mr. Sharpe translates, 'until he come to Shiloh,' which the Revisers allow as an alternative rendering, and both he and Mr. Wellbeloved anticipated the two other improvements admitted in the New Version; the latter remarking in a note, that the New Testament does not speak of Christ under the name of Shiloh, and that it would be difficult to show that the position of Judah was in any sense like that here described at the time of Christ's coming. That 'Judah maintained its corporate existence as a tribe until the coming of the Prince of Peace,' which is the explanation of the Quarterly Reviewer, will probably appear to ordinary readers a poor fulfilment of so imperial a prediction, even if the facts were not against it.

## NUM. xxiv. 17—19.

| | |
|---|---|
| I shall see him, but not now: I shall behold him, but not nigh: there shall come a Star out of Jacob, and a Sceptre shall rise out of Israel, and | I see him, but not now: I behold him, but not nigh: there shall come forth a star out of Jacob, and a sceptre shall rise out of Israel, and shall smite |

*Authorized Version.*

shall smite the corners of Moab, and destroy all the children of Sheth. And Edom shall be a possession, Seir also shall be a possession for his enemies; and Israel shall do valiantly. Out of Jacob shall come he that shall have dominion, and shall destroy him that remaineth of the city.

*Revised Version.*

through the corners of Moab, and break down all the sons of tumult.* And Edom shall be a possession, Seir also shall be a possession, *which were* his enemies; while Israel doeth valiantly. And out of Jacob shall one have dominion, and shall destroy the remnant from the city.

[* Or, *Sheth.*

It has been noticed in the Review article above quoted, that the Authorized Version recognized the Messianic character of this prophecy by spelling the words Star and Sceptre with capitals, and the writer complains that a portion of the Revisers (i.e. two-thirds of them at least: see their rules) wished to minimize the Messianic prophecies in the text of the Old Testament. The translation here given is singularly like that of Mr. Wellbeloved. He held that the reference was to David's victories over Moab (2 Sam. viii. 2, 14).

### Ex. iii. 14, 15.

And God said unto Moses, I AM THAT I AM: and he said, Thus shalt thou say unto the children of Israel, I AM hath sent me unto you. And God said moreover unto Moses, Thus shalt thou say unto the children of Israel, The LORD God of your fathers . . .

And God said unto Moses, I AM THAT I AM:* and he said, Thus shalt thou say unto the children of Israel, I AM† hath sent me unto you. And God said moreover unto Moses, Thus shalt thou say unto the children of Israel, The LORD,‡ the God of your fathers . . .

[* Or, *I am because I am;* or, *I am who am;* or, *I will be that I will be.*    † Or, *I will be,* Heb. *Ehyeh.*    ‡ Heb. *Jehovah,* from the same root as *Ehyeh.*

Mr. Wellbeloved translated, 'I WILL BE WHAT I WILL be,' and so later, 'I WILL BE hath sent me,' and (*v.* 15), 'HE WHO WILL BE, the God of your fathers.' The Revisers allow that this at least may be the proper rendering, and thus that the name was not given as a definition of the Divine Essence, but as a token of God's faithfulness to his promises ; or, as in *v.* 12, a renewal of his assurance of protection, 'Certainly I will be with thee.'

When, therefore, in John viii. 58, Jesus says, 'Before Abraham was I am,' a phrase which occurs repeatedly in this Gospel for 'I am he,' i.e. the Messiah of Divine appointment,[1] it is hardly to be supposed that he refers to the text in Ex. iii. 14 above quoted, where the verb is in the future, not in the present tense. In Mark xiii. 6, where the Authorized Version reads, 'many shall come in my name, saying, I am *Christ*,' the Revisers use the more natural expression suggested by the original, and put, 'saying, I am *he*.'

---

Ps. ii. 12.

| *Authorized Version.* | *Revised Version.* |
|---|---|
| Kiss the Son, lest he be angry, and ye perish from the way, when his wrath is kindled but a little. | Kiss the son,* lest he be angry, and ye perish in the way, for his wrath will† soon be kindled. |
| | [* Some ancient versions render, *Lay hold of (or receive) instruction ;* others, *Worship in purity.*   † Or, *may.* |

The Edinburgh Reviewer[2] objects to the Revisers printing 'the son' with a small s, as they have also done just before in *v.* 7, 'Thou art my son, this day have I begotten thee,' so obscuring the Messianic intention, and leaving the passage

---

[1] It is so translated in this very chapter, *vv.* 24, 28, 'except ye believe that I am *he*,' 'then shall ye know that I am *he*.' The Improved Version has the translation suggested here in the margin, 'Before Abraham was born.'

[2] 'Edinburgh Review,' October, 1885.

G 2

to be applied only to the Hebrew monarch, to whom, as
all agree, the psalm primarily refers.    Mr. Wellbeloved
translated, ' Reverence,' or ' Do homage sincerely,' remarking
that in pure Hebrew the word which he renders 'sincerely'
never means ' son,' though even if it had that meaning in
this place, the son could only have been the anointed king
(*v.* 2) to whom Jehovah had plainly given this exalted title
(*v.* 7).   This text is cited here chiefly on account of the note
suggesting a revision more in harmony with the context.
Perhaps the true sense corresponds with the previous ' Be
instructed' of *v.* 10.   In any case, there would seem to be no
reference in *v.* 12 to ' the Son.'   It is the wrath of the LORD
(see *v.* 11) with which the revolting nations are threatened ;
and every reader may observe that the LORD is the proper
subject of both the 11th and 12th verses.

----

'Thy throne, O God, is for ever and ever,' Ps. xlv. 6.   On
this text there is a note in the Revised margin, ' or, *thy
throne is the throne of God,*' &c.   This is of great importance
as throwing light upon the quotation of the passage in Heb.
i. 8, in application to the Son, where the same ambiguity
is found in the Greek, and of course the same alternative
translation must be understood to be admissible.

Two other points deserve notice in regard to this quotation
in the Epistle.   In the text the Revisers properly correct
' Unto the Son *he saith,*' to ' Of the Son,' and they insert at
' the sceptre of thy kingdom' the note that ' The two oldest
Greek manuscripts read ' his.'   This variation may be,
probably is, wrong, but the reader may judge from it how
the transcribers understood the passage, and will observe
that the Quarterly Reviewer has not sufficient ground for
characterizing the marginal note to Ps. xlv. 6, as a contra-
diction of an inspired interpretation of the verse.

The correction ' of' instead of ' to the Son' covers also
the subsequent quotation (Heb. i. 10—12), 'And, Thou LORD
in the beginning,' &c., from another Psalm (cii. 25—27).

Whatever the idea was in the mind of the writer, he does not affirm that this Psalm was addressed to the Son. And if with the margin of the Old Testament Revisers we read in the preceding passage, 'Thy throne is the throne of God for ever,' the connection of thought in the second quotation becomes clear: the throne of the Son shall be as enduring as God's eternity. See the last verse of Ps. cii., which draws a similar inference from this Divine attribute.

Supposing, however, that the expression, 'O God,' is applied to the Son, it should be remembered that the Hebrew word is Elohim, the plural name which has been supposed to imply the Trinity when used in the Old Testament. But Elohim can hardly mean three persons, and, at the same time, be used for only one of the three.

---

In a preceding verse of the Psalm (xlv. 3), the Revisers make a correction that deserves notice, since the addition of the adverb 'most,' which appears in the Authorized Version in italics, to show that it was an addition, has been understood to favour the Messianic application of the whole Psalm. Instead of 'Gird thy sword upon thy thigh, O *most* mighty, with thy glory and thy majesty,' we now read, 'Gird thy sword upon thy thigh, O mighty one, thy glory and thy majesty.'

---

### PROV. viii. 22.

| *Authorized Version.* | *Revised Version.* |
|---|---|
| The LORD possessed me in the beginning of his way, before his works of old. | The LORD possessed* me in† the beginning of his way, before‡ his works of old. |
| | [* Or, *formed*.  † Or, *as*.  ‡ Or, *the first of*. |

The passage may therefore be read, 'The Lord formed me as the beginning of his way, the first of his works of old,' which, if it be understood of a person, is obviously very far from supporting the doctrine of certain orthodox Church authorities. Upon the verb 'formed,' the Arians of the fourth century much relied, as distinctly asserting that Christ was a created being, and therefore not co-eternal and consubstantial with the Father. The Quarterly Reviewer complains that the Revisers have suggested this Arian interpretation, and he refers on the contrary to 'the judgment of Catholic antiquity' to show that the true rendering 'conveys the sublime doctrine of the eternal generation of the Second Person in the Trinity.' This is probably one of the marginal notes in which he says the Revisers 'seem to start with a prejudice against the Christian faith,' meaning, of course, the Reviewer's own ideas of what constitutes the Christian faith.

---

### MIC. v. 2.

| *Authorized Version.* | *Revised Version.* |
|---|---|
| Out of thee shall he come forth unto me that is to be ruler in Israel; whose goings forth have been from of old, from everlasting. | Out of thee shall one come forth unto me that is to be ruler in Israel; whose goings forth are from of old, from everlasting.* |
| | [* Or, *from ancient days.* |

Mr. S. Sharpe translates, 'from former times, from days of old,' and Mr. Wellbeloved, 'whose origin is of old, from ancient times,' either as being of the family of David, or as foretold in ancient prophecy. The margin certainly gives little support to the well-known inference from this passage as to the Son's eternal generation.

---

### Is. liii. 8.

| He was taken from prison and from judgment; and who shall declare his generation? for he was cut off out of the land of the living. | By* oppression and judgment he was taken away; and as for his generation,† who among them considered that he was cut off out of the land of the living? |
|---|---|
| | [* Or, *From.*    † Or, *and his life who shall recount? for he was cut off,* &c. |

The text of the New Version in this passage gives no countenance to the idea that the prophet was referring to the mysterious, eternal generation of the Second Person of the Trinity. The translation is substantially the same as that of Dr. G. R. Noyes, as also of Dr. G. Vance Smith, 'Who of his generation considereth that,' &c. Bishop Lowth translates, ' His manner of life who would declare ?' which corresponds with the Revisers' margin.

In the second verse of this chapter may be observed a correction which makes the whole description of the Servant of God more consistently historical. Instead of 'he shall grow up,' the text now reads, 'he grew up;' and 'when we see him' is put in place of 'when we shall see him;' the margin giving the variation, 'or, that we should look upon him.'

---

### DAN. vii. 13.

| *Authorized Version.* | *Revised Version.* |
|---|---|
| Behold, one like the Son of man came with the clouds of heaven, and came to the Ancient of days. | Behold there came with the clouds of heaven one like unto a son of man, and he came even to the ancient of days. |

Referring to *v.* 9, in the New Version, we read, ' I beheld till thrones were placed, and one that was ancient of days did sit,' where the Old Version has, 'and the Ancient of days.' The symbol of a son of man, set in contrast with the great beasts or kingdoms of the prophecy, is interpreted in the context as representing the Jewish people, the saints of the Most High, to whom was to be given an everlasting kingdom. A new turn is given to the expression in Matt. xxiv. 30, and xxvi. 64, but the Revisers have not thought proper to anticipate this application of the text, as was done in the Authorized Version, by the usual capital letter which marks a proper name.

---

## HAG. ii. 7.

| *Authorized Version.* | *Revised Version.* |
|---|---|
| And the desire of all nations shall come. | And the desirable things* of all nations shall come.<br><br>[* Or. *the things desired* (Heb. *desire*) *of all nations shall come.* |

This is word for word the rendering of Mr. Wellbeloved. Dr. Noyes says, 'the precious things.' The context shows that the meaning is 'the treasures of all nations' (to use Mr. Sharpe's expression), which should be gathered in the temple then building in Jerusalem. The Quarterly Reviewer suspects that this variation also proceeds from a prejudice 'against all Messianic prophecy.'[1] But the Revisers have simply made an honest translation. There is clearly no reference to a person.

---

## Is. lix. 20.

| | |
|---|---|
| And the Redeemer shall come to Zion, and unto them that turn from transgression in Jacob. | And a redeemer shall come to Zion, and unto them that turn from transgression in Jacob. |

In the Authorized Version, the Redeemer (so printed) appeared to point clearly to him of whom Paul seems to have been thinking when (Rom. xi. 26) he quoted this passage ('There shall come out of Sion the Deliverer;[2] he shall turn away ungodliness from Jacob'), but from the Septuagint, not the Hebrew text. The Old Greek Version materially altered the sense in the latter clause. The Revisers have kept faithfully to the Hebrew, and translate it literally. Thus the context is allowed weight, which shows that the

---

[1] A recent writer, who says of the older version, 'We would fain retain it if we could,' adds that 'almost every scholar of repute admits that it is simply an impossible rendering of the original.'—'Old Testament Revision,' by Alex. Roberts, D.D., 1883, p. 88.

[2] It is worth while remarking that in Acts vii. 35, where Stephen says of Moses, 'The same did God send to be both a ruler and a deliverer,' the margin states that the original word means 'a redeemer.'

prophet was speaking of the nearer deliverance of which the whole of the latter portion of Isaiah is full.

---

### Is. vii. 14.

| *Authorized Version.* | *Revised Version.* |
|---|---|
| Behold a virgin shall conceive, and bear a son, and shall call his name Immanuel. | Behold a* virgin† shall conceive and bear‡ a son, and shall call his name Immanuel.§ |
| | [* Or, *the.*     † Or, *maiden.* ‡ Or, *is with child and beareth.* § That is, *God is with us.* |

The marginal notes here are very instructive, though the old Version is retained in the text. If in the second note is given not merely another term synonymous with the word in the text, then the definite article supplied in the first probably suggests the true sense, pointing to a particular person, a certain young woman, as has been maintained.[1] This is favoured by the introduction of the definite article in the Revision of Matt. i. 23, 'Behold the virgin.' But in this indicated variation the Quarterly Reviewer suspects something anti-Messianic, and opposed to the Deity of the Saviour. What it is he does not explain.

The third note is specially important. Dr. G. V. Smith renders to the same effect 'hath conceived and shall bear,' and Bp. Lowth 'conceiveth and beareth.' See Gen. xvi. 11, where a similar expression occurs.

It should be further remarked that the Revisers give the correct translation of the name Immanuel, after the example of similar names compounded with the word God. This interpretation is given by Mr. S. Sharpe in the quotation from the prophet in Matt. i. 23, as it is here by the Old

---

[1] For example, by Dr. S. Davidson, who says of the Hebrew word rendered *maiden* that 'a virgin proper is not its primary meaning.'—'On a Fresh Revision of the English Old Testament,' 1873.

Testament Revisers, though the New Testament Revisers omit it. Similar appellations occur, for example, in Ezek. xlviii. 35, 'And the name of the city from that day shall be, "The LORD is there," and Ex. xvii. 15, 'The LORD hath sworn.'

In the following passage the Revisers have inserted in the text the proper rendering of such names, relegating to the margin the Authorized form :

### JER. xxiii. 6.

| *Authorized Version.* | *Revised Version.* |
|---|---|
| And this is his name whereby he shall be called, THE LORD OUR RIGHTEOUSNESS. | And this is his name whereby he shall be called, The LORD is our righteousness. |

In Jer. xxxiii. 16, where this name is repeated, it is given to Jerusalem. The Revisers refer to this text, which makes the same general prediction in a different form, in justification of their correction. Here is the passage :

### JER. xxxiii. 16.

| | |
|---|---|
| And Jerusalem shall dwell safely, and this is the name wherewith she shall be called, The LORD our righteousness. | And Jerusalem shall dwell safely, and this is the name whereby she shall be called, The LORD is our righteousness. |

---

### DAN. ix. 26.

| | |
|---|---|
| And after threescore and two weeks shall Messiah be cut off, but not for himself. | And after the threescore and two weeks shall the anointed one be cut off, and shall have nothing.* |
| | [* Or, *there shall be none belonging to him.* |

So, as in this margin, Mr. J. Scott Porter rendered the last clause as meaning that he should have no successors, 'and none shall be left unto him.' Mr. Sharpe says, 'and nothing shall remain to him.' The popular idea of one who should be called Messiah dying as a substitute for others, was not in the original, and it appears no longer in the Revised version of this passage. It is worthy of note that the translation now adopted in the text, 'shall have nothing,' appears in the old Authorized margin.

---

### DAN. ix. 25.

| *Authorized Version.* | *Revised Version.* |
|---|---|
| Unto the Messiah, the Prince. | Unto the anointed one,* the prince. |
| | [* Or, *Messiah, the prince;* or, *an anointed one, a prince.* |

With this correction, the 'Messiah' as a proper name, indeed the term itself in any sense, disappears from the text, greatly to the annoyance of the Quarterly Reviewer, in the only Old Testament passage where it occurred, being relegated to the margin, which reads, 'or, *Messiah the prince;* or, *an anointed one, a prince.*' Mr. J. Scott Porter, in the Revised Translation of 1862, gave the same sense, 'until a prince shall be anointed,' and Mr. Sharpe 'an anointed ruler.' To whom the expression points becomes thus a question of history, not theology. 'Obviously,' says the Quarterly Reviewer here, 'the Revisers reject any Messianic reference whatever, as they do not even spell anointed one or prince with capital letters.'

In the preceding verse (Dan. ix. 24) an important change of the kind just adverted to is made in the Revised Version. Instead of 'the most Holy,' which has been usually understood to mean Christ, we observe the different form, 'the most holy.' The marginal notes should be specially considered. 'Seventy weeks are decreed upon thy people and upon thy holy city, to finish (marg. or, *to restrain*) transgression (or, *the transgression*), and to make (another reading is, *to seal up*) an end of sins, and to make reconciliation for (or, *purge away*) iniquity, and to bring in everlasting righteousness, and to seal up vision and prophecy (Heb. *prophet*), and to anoint the most holy (or, *a most holy place*).' Mr. J. Scott Porter so translated this final clause, 'to anoint the most holy place.'

---

## DAN. iii. 25.

| *Authorized Version.* | *Revised Version.* |
|---|---|
| And the form of the fourth is like the Son of God. | And the aspect of the fourth is like a son of the gods. |

This was the only passage in the Authorized Old Testament Version in which the title 'the Son of God' occurred. Mr. J. Scott Porter did not venture so far as the Revisers have done : he rendered the phrase, 'a Son of God.' In *v.* 28, the king speaks of this fourth being as an angel sent by the God of Shadrach, Meshach, and Abed-nego to deliver them. The centurion, in Matt. xxvii. 54, uses the phrase, as Thomas Wintle observes, in the same manner, with reference to Christ. The Revised Version translates that passage with the Authorized, 'Truly this was the Son of God.' But there is no article in the Greek, and in the marginal note we read, 'or, *a Son of God.*'

---

## MAL. iii. 1.

| | |
|---|---|
| Behold I will send my messenger, and he shall prepare the way before me, and the Lord whom ye seek shall suddenly come to his temple, even the messenger of the covenant whom ye delight in ; behold, he shall come, saith the LORD of hosts. | Behold I send my messenger, and he shall prepare the way before me, and the Lord whom ye seek shall suddenly come to his temple, and * the messenger† of the covenant whom ye delight in ; behold, he cometh, saith the LORD of hosts. |
| | [* Or, *even.*    † Or, *angel.* |

'Even the messenger' is thus placed in the margin, and for 'the messenger' the alternative rendering is suggested of 'the angel.' Mr. Wellbeloved also has 'and,' marking this as the beginning of a separate clause. But if 'the Angel of the covenant' be, according to either version, the same as 'the Lord whom ye seek,' the reader may be reminded of a similar usage in Gen. xlviii. 16, where 'the God which fed me' is clearly further designated 'the Angel which redeemed me from all evil.' In neither case is there even an 'adumbration' of a personality distinct from, and yet the same as, the LORD of hosts, the speaker in the present text; while of course a messenger, if that be the right translation, must be distinguished from the LORD who was to send him.

ZECH. xii. 10.

| *Authorized Version.* | *Revised Version.* |
|---|---|
| And they shall look upon me whom they have pierced, and they shall mourn for him, &c. | And they shall look upon me* whom they have pierced, and they shall mourn for him, &c. |
| | [* According to some MSS. *him.* |

This text has been assumed to identify the Saviour who was pierced, with Jehovah, who here speaks. Archbishop Newcome, Mr. Wellbeloved, and Mr. Sharpe, followed the different reading, 'him whom they pierced,' and the Revisers enable the reader to infer that this was not without good critical grounds. The author of John (xix. 37) certainly understood the passage thus. His quotation reads, 'They shall look on him whom they pierced.'

Ps. xxii. 16.

| They pierced my hands and my feet. | They* pierced my hands and my feet. |
|---|---|
| | [* So the Sept., Vulg. and Syr. According to other ancient versions, *They bound.* The Heb. text, as pointed, reads, *like a lion.* |

"This passage speaks," says the Quarterly Reviewer, "of the crucifixion of the Saviour. The Revisers suffer the received translation to stand, but they entirely evacuate its meaning by their marginal note." The verse is one, he adds, "of vast importance."

## Is. xxvi. 19.

| *Authorized Version.* | *Revised Version.* |
|---|---|
| Thy dead *men* shall live, *together with* my dead body shall they arise.  Awake and sing, ye that dwell in dust: for thy dew is as the dew of herbs, and the earth shall cast forth her dead. | Thy dead shall live, my dead bodies shall arise.  Awake and sing, ye that dwell in the dust; for thy dew is as the dew of herbs, and the earth shall cast forth the dead.* |

[* Or, *the shades*, Heb. *Rephaim*.

This has been understood to anticipate the New Testament view of the saints rising from the dead 'together with' Christ.  It is now left to be interpreted by its own context as a figurative description of the fulfilment on earth and in time of the grand promises to the Jewish nation.

## Job xix. 25.

| | |
|---|---|
| For I know that my redeemer liveth, and that he shall stand at the latter day upon the earth : and *though* after my skin *worms* destroy this *body*, yet in my flesh shall I see God. | But I know that my redeemer* liveth, and that he shall stand up at the last upon the earth :† and‡ after my skin hath been thus destroyed, yet from§ my flesh shall I see God, whom I shall see for myself,‖ and mine eyes shall behold, and not another.¶ |

[* Or, *vindicator*, Heb. *goel*. † Heb. *dust*. ‡ Or, *and after my skin hath been destroyed, this shall be, even from*, &c.; or, *and though after my skin this body be destroyed, yet from*, &c. § Or, *without*. ‖ Or, *on my side*. ¶ Or, *as a stranger*.

Though 'redeemer' is retained here, the reader is instructed in the margin that the Hebrew word means a 'vindicator.'  Mr. Wellbeloved says, 'avenger,' as the term is rendered in other places, e.g. 'avenger of blood' (Deut.

xix. 6). In neither sense is it applicable to Christ. Had the Revisers thought otherwise, they would have printed the word with a capital, their usual practice in such cases. In the margin will be found Mr. Wellbeloved's rendering of the following verse, though it is not given in the text. Instead of 'whom I shall see for myself, and mine eyes shall behold, and not another,' he points the moral of the whole passage by translating the verse, 'whom I shall behold on my side, and mine eyes shall see, but not estranged *from me.*' The notion of a resurrection of the body at the call of the Redeemer, which this text has long been thought to support, is thus no longer perceptible there; but, on the other hand, the essentially Jewish belief that Job would assuredly be justified in God's good time, notwithstanding all he might yet be called to suffer.

### References to the Old Testament in the New.

The following passages taken from the New Testament make specific reference to the Old, and may therefore be considered here. The proper name 'Joshua' is given in Acts vii. 45 and Heb. iv. 8, where the Authorized Version had 'Jesus.' The amendment, though slight, was worth making, to avoid possible misconception.

### JOHN xii. 41.

| *Authorized Version.* | *Revised Version.* |
|---|---|
| These things said Esaias, when he saw his glory, and spake of him. | These things said Isaiah, because he saw his glory; and he spake of him. |

Griesbach's text reads here 'because,' not 'when.' John is quoting two passages from the book of Isaiah, one in chapter liii. and the other in chapter vi. The latter forms a kind of introduction of the prophet to his office, and it opens with the statement that he saw Jehovah sitting upon a throne. It has been therefore inferred that Jesus was

Jehovah, and the translation of the Authorized Version favoured the idea by connecting the prophecies quoted with the opening of the prophet's commission. Esaias said these things at the time of his seeing—'when he saw.' 'Because he saw' is a better reading, and gives a sense not pointing to the one quotation only, that of chapter vi. It corresponds, in fact, with the similar foreseeing attributed to the father of the faithful in John viii. 56, 'Your father Abraham rejoiced to see my day; and he saw it and was glad,' where the Revisers suggest in their margin the probably true interpretation : they say, 'or, *rejoiced that he should see.*' Compare Heb. xi. 13, 'not having received the promises, but having seen and greeted them from afar' (R.V.).

---

### GAL. iii. 17.

| *Authorized Version.* | *Revised Version.* |
|---|---|
| Now this I say, that the Covenant that was confirmed before of God in Christ, the law ... cannot disannul. | Now this I say: A covenant confirmed beforehand by God, the law ... doth not disannul. |

'In Christ' or 'unto Christ' would seem to have been a gloss, and it is now omitted as having no MS. authority. It is one example out of many of expressions which, so introduced, have given a certain mystic character to these allusions to the Old Testament beyond what the New Testament writers intended.

---

### I COR. x. 9.

| | |
|---|---|
| Neither let us tempt Christ, as some of them also tempted, and were destroyed of serpents. | Neither let us tempt the Lord,*as some of them tempted, and perished by the serpents.<br><br>[* Some ancient authorities read, *Christ.* |

This is the precise expression in Ex. xvii. 2, 'Wherefore do ye tempt the LORD?' See also Deut. vi. 16. With the marginal note should be compared a similar note on the text in Jude (*v.* 5), 'how that the Lord, having saved the people out of the land of Egypt, afterward destroyed them that believed not.' The note is, ' Many very ancient authorities read, *Jesus.*' The second and third centuries, says Dr. Scrivener, did more to corrupt the text than all the centuries succeeding. This was in fact the period when the doctrine of the Deity of Christ was gathering strength, and becoming more distinctly formed.

In another case, in Rom. x. 17, the two oldest authorities agree in the reading which is given in the Revised Version, ' So belief *cometh* of hearing, and hearing by the word of Christ,' where the Authorized Version has 'the word of God.' Dean Alford says here, '' God' has probably been a rationalizing correction, to suit better the sense of the prophecy.' But it is quite as likely that Christ was put instead of God to suit the maturing orthodoxy of the time. There is no doctrinal difficulty in the text either way, but it is more in Paul's manner to speak of ' the word of God' in so referring to the ancient Scriptures. Compare, however, with this a similar change, which may be noted here, though not properly belonging to this chapter. In Eph. v. 21, where the Authorized Version reads, ' subjecting yourselves one to another in the fear of God,' the Revised Version has, ' in the fear of Christ.' Dean Alford calls this ' an uncommon phrase,' which, however, he inserts in his text in deference to ' all our oldest MSS.'

---

HEB. xi. 25.

| *Authorized Version.* | *Revised Version.* |
|---|---|
| Choosing rather to suffer affliction with the people of God, than to enjoy the pleasures of sin for a season: | Choosing rather to be evil entreated with the people of God, than to enjoy the pleasures of sin for a season: |
| 26. Esteeming the reproach of Christ* greater riches than the treasures in Egypt. | 26. Accounting the reproach of Christ* greater riches than the treasures of Egypt. |
| [* Or, *for Christ.* | [* Or, *the Christ.* |

H

The margin suggests what is probably the true sense. It is the reproach of the people of God. The people of Israel are spoken of by the prophet who was sent to Eli as 'mine anointed' (1 Sam. ii. 35), where the Septuagint uses this word, 'my Christ.' So Ps. cv. 15, the Revisers read, 'Touch not mine anointed ones,' speaking of Abraham and his seed, the children of Jacob, 'his chosen ones' (*v.* 6). Here also the Sept. reads, 'my Christs.' Compare the following, which, again, the Sept. translates, 'thy Christ.'

### HABAK. iii. 13.

| *Authorized Version.* | *Revised Version.* |
|---|---|
| Thou wentest forth for the salvation of thy people, *even* for salvation with thine anointed. | Thou wentest* forth for the salvation of thy people, for the salvation of† thine anointed. |
| | [* Or, *art come.*       † Or, *for salvation* (or, *victory*) *with.* |

So Mr. Wellbeloved translated, 'For the deliverance of thine anointed.'

---

### *Supposed Proofs of Christ's Pre-existence.*

#### JOHN i. 15.

| | |
|---|---|
| He that cometh after me is preferred before me, for he was before me. | He that cometh after me is become before me: for he was before me.* |
| | [* Or, *first in regard of me.* |

That is, 'my Superior,' or, 'Principal,' to use Mr. Cappe's expression, which was adopted in the Improved Version; as the other Gospels say, 'is mightier than I.' The note gives in fact the key to the only consistent interpretation of the phrase. Having received a higher commission, Jesus would naturally be expected by John to take the higher place.

---

## John vi. 33.

| *Authorized Version.* | *Revised Version.* |
|---|---|
| For the bread of God is he which cometh down from heaven, and giveth life unto the world. | For the bread of God is that which cometh down out of heaven, and giveth life unto the world. |

So reads the Improved Version—a grammatical improvement, making, however, little doctrinal difference, since elsewhere, as in verse 38, Jesus is represented as saying, 'I am come down from heaven' (R.V.), and the Jews are reported (v. 41) to have understood him to affirm that he was 'the bread which came down out of heaven' (R.V.).

Of more importance is the marginal note to John iii. 13, because the being spoken of there is clearly 'the man Christ Jesus;' and whether in Christ there were two natures or not, the Divine Nature is never called 'the Son of Man.' At this passage, which reads, 'Even the Son of Man which is in heaven,' the Revisers inform us that 'many ancient authorities omit, *which is in heaven.*' A note in the Improved Version intimated that this clause was wanting 'in some of the best copies.' See John i. 18, where the same form is used, not 'who is,' but the participial form which approaches nearly to our 'he,' or 'who being' in the bosom of the Father, that is, in intimate sympathy and communion with him, according to a well-understood Jewish figure.

---

## 1 Cor. xv. 47.

| The first man is of the earth, earthy. The second man is the Lord from heaven. | The first man is of the earth, earthy; the second man is of heaven. |
|---|---|

The preposition is the same in both clauses. The contrast in the Apostle's mind between the natural and the spiritual, or the earthly and the heavenly, is now brought out in accordance with his previous argument. The expression, 'the Lord from heaven,' if understood to imply Christ's pre-existence in a divine or superhuman nature, would scarcely· harmonize with Paul's conception of his having been 'determined to be the Son of God by the resurrection of the dead' (Rom. i. 4, R.V. note on 'declared to be,' Gr. *determined*).   The same view is attributed to the Apostle in Acts xiii. 33 : 'the promise made unto the Fathers . . . God hath fulfilled . . . in that he raised up Jesus, as also it is written in the second Psalm, Thou art my Son, this day have I begotten thee.'

───────────

HEB. ii. 16.

| *Authorized Version.* | *Revised Version.* |
|---|---|
| For verily he took not on him *the nature* of angels, but he took on him the seed of Abraham. | For verily not of angels doth he take hold, but he taketh hold of the seed of Abraham. |

That is, 'to help,' 'to take by the hand.'   The insertion of the words in italics, 'the nature,' is the more remarkable in the Version of 1611, as its margin gives substantially the new rendering, the specific sense of which is indicated also in v. 18, 'he is able to succour them that are tempted.'[1]   The improvement in the translation is not only of importance in itself, but it clears away what Bishop C. H. Terrot declared to have been 'one of the greatest errors in our Authorized Version.'

═══════════

### *Christ's Resurrection.*

In about two dozen places in the Acts and Epistles it is affirmed that Jesus was raised, not by any inherent power of his own, but by the act of God.   Amendments like the following are not therefore without importance.   The expres-

───────────

[1] The Improved Version presents a similar view of this passage, but refers in a note to an ingenious exposition in the Theological Repository (Vol. V. p. 164), according to which it was the fear of death to which, not angels, but men only were subject, and the translation would then be, not 'he,' but 'it.'

sion still occurs very naturally in a few passages, that Jesus 'rose' from the dead, but obviously in the same sense in which it is said of the dead in Christ (1 Thess. iv. 16) that they 'shall rise first.'

## 2 COR. iv. 14.

| *Authorized Version.* | *Revised Version.* |
|---|---|
| Knowing that he which raised up the Lord Jesus shall raise up us also by Jesus, and shall present us with you. | Knowing that he which raised up the Lord Jesus* shall raise up us also with Jesus, and shall present us with you.<br><br>[* Some ancient authorities omit *the Lord.* |

The manner of the raising up is thus argued to be the same for all. We are raised with Jesus, not by Jesus. (See 1 Thess. iv. 14, 'will God bring with him.') It is in each case the direct act of God.

## MATT. xx. 19.

| And the third day he shall rise again. | And the third day he shall be raised up. |
|---|---|

Using the same language, Jesus says, 'But after I am raised up (not 'am risen again'), I will go before you into Galilee' (Matt. xxvi. 32, R.V.). Paul writes in the same manner—

## ROM. viii. 34.

| It is Christ that died, yea rather, that is risen again. | It is* Christ Jesus that died, yea rather, that was raised from the dead.<br><br>[* Or, *shall Christ Jesus*, &c. |
|---|---|

## 1 COR. xv. 4.

| And that he rose again the third day. | And that he hath been raised on the third day. |
|---|---|

## 1 COR. xv. 20.

| But now is Christ risen from the dead, *and* become the first-fruits of them that slept. | But now hath Christ been raised from the dead, the first-fruits of them that are asleep. |
|---|---|

And so throughout the chapter. These passages throw light upon the remaining texts in this section—

JOHN x. 18.

| *Authorized Version.* | *Revised Version.* |
|---|---|
| I have power to lay it [my life] down, and I have power to take it again. This commandment have I received of my Father. | I have power\* to lay it down, and I have power\* to take it again. This commandment received I from my Father.<br>[\* Or, *right*. |

The word so rendered 'power' or 'right,' is translated 'authority' in other places, as it is in this text in the Improved Version. Jesus makes no claim even here to any right or power but what the Father had given him. And if he could say of the temple of his body, as the Evangelist explains, 'Destroy this temple, and in three days I will raise it up' (John ii. 19), it is to be observed that the expression the writer then uses in further speaking of this is not, as in the Authorized Version, 'when therefore he was risen from the dead,' but 'when he was raised' (*v.* 22, R.V.).

The correction in the following passage is not only one of considerable theological interest, but it relieves a Biblical difficulty, while implying a view of the objects of Christ's death which was very familiar to the older Unitarians. They looked upon the resuscitation of Christ as the Divine method of bringing 'life and immortality to light,' God having begotten us again 'unto a living hope by the resurrection of Jesus Christ from the dead' (1 Pet. i. 3, R.V.).

ACTS xxvi. 23.

| | |
|---|---|
| That he should be the first that should rise from the dead, and should show light unto the people, and to the Gentiles. | That he first by the resurrection of the dead should proclaim light both to the people and to the Gentiles. |

The following correction also deserves notice : it was anticipated in the Improved Version—

ROM. xiv. 9.

| | |
|---|---|
| To this end Christ both died, and rose, and revived, that he might be Lord both of the dead and living. | To this end Christ died and lived *again*, that he might be Lord of both the dead and the living. |

# SOME SIGNIFICANT NAMES GIVEN TO JESUS.

## LUKE ii. 43.

| *Authorized Version.* | *Revised Version.* |
|---|---|
| The child Jesus tarried behind in Jerusalem, and Joseph and his mother knew not of it. | The boy Jesus tarried behind in Jerusalem, and his parents knew it not. |

## LUKE ii. 33.

| And Joseph and his mother marvelled at those things which were spoken of him. | And his father and his mother[1] were marvelling at the things which were spoken concerning him. |
|---|---|

The Improved Version also makes the latter of these two corrections. Mr. Sharpe supposed that a later transcriber had noticed the inconsistency here with the account of the parentage of Jesus in Matthew, and endeavoured to remove it by not speaking of Joseph as his father; but the same difficulty occurs in the third Gospel, in which also the story of the nativity is related in a way that does not harmonize with the texts just given. The accounts came probably from different sources. Yet observe how naturally the narrative in Luke ii. 48 records the words of Mary, 'Thy father and I sought thee sorrowing.'

---

*The Son, the Son of Man.*

## MATT. xxiv. 36.

| But of that day and hour knoweth no man, no, not the Angels of heaven, but my Father only. | But of that day and hour knoweth no one, not even the angels of heaven, neither the Son,* but the Father only. |
|---|---|
| | [* Many authorities, some ancient, omit *neither the Son*. |

---

[1] In 1 Tim. ii. 15, 'she shall be saved in childbearing,' is altered by the Revisers to 'through the childbearing,' which has been supposed to allude to the Incarnation of the Godhead in the birth of Christ. But they note in the margin, 'or, *her childbearing*,' which may be understood more naturally to recall the text in Gen. iii. 16.

That the corresponding passage in Mark (xiii. 32) had this emphatic declaration of the imperfect knowledge of the Son of Man has been considered an argument in favour of its priority to the first Gospel, but the momentous statement now appears in both Gospels. The Improved Version noted at this place in Matthew that the words were found in some MSS. and Versions of good repute. Certainly they were more likely to be omitted from a MS. than inserted afresh even from another Gospel. It is the more noteworthy that the Revisers place them here in the text. Some of the Fathers were much perplexed at the statement that the Son's knowledge was limited, but they created their own difficulty by assuming that Christ was speaking of himself as God the Son. On the other hand, even the common Scriptural phrase, the 'Son of God,' does not occur in the chapter, while 'Son of Man' does appear in the immediate context. But whether as Son of God or Son of Man, Jesus clearly affirmed that he had not been granted the knowledge in question.

*The Term Son of God.*

In Matt. xiv. 33, the simple translation would be, 'Of a truth thou art a son of God.' The Revisers follow the Authorized Version, 'thou art the Son of God,' giving no indication that the noun has no article in the Greek. Compare with this, Mark xv. 39, 'Truly this man was the Son of God,' and the parallel text in Matt. xxvii. 54, with the marginal note, 'or, *a son of God*,' the Greek being the same in each case (see p. 92). In these texts, considering who were the speakers, the more simple meaning of the term is surely the more natural one, but even in a passage like the following the original reads, 'a son of God.' The angel says—

## LUKE i. 35.

| *Authorized Version.* | *Revised Version.* |
| --- | --- |
| Therefore also that holy thing which shall be born of thee shall be called the Son of God. | Wherefore also that which is to be born shall be called holy, the Son of God. |

------

Although in various passages the name 'Son of God' is applied in the New Testament in a special sense to Jesus Christ, it should be remarked that it is employed very freely in various parts of the Bible in other applications. For example, in Hos. i. 10, the phrase is applied to God's people, 'Ye are the sons of the living God.' The same use of the expression in the New Testament is well brought out by the Revisers in the correction of the following passages. Note also the punctuation in the third text, which shows the true sense to be, 'sons of God in Christ Jesus, through faith.' The first text is a quotation of the passage in Hosea—

## ROM. ix. 26.

| There shall they be called the children of the living God. | There shall they be called sons of the living God. |
| --- | --- |

## EPH. i. 5.

| Having predestinated us unto the adoption of children by Jesus Christ to himself. | Having foreordained us unto adoption as sons through Jesus Christ unto himself. |
| --- | --- |

## GAL. iii. 26.

| For ye are all the children of God by faith in Christ Jesus. | For ye are all sons of God, through faith, in Christ Jesus. |
| --- | --- |

The following is an example of the New Testament use of the term after the manner of the prophetic text above quoted :

### LUKE xx. 36.

| *Authorized Version.* | *Revised Version.* |
|---|---|
| Neither can they die any more ; for they are equal unto the angels, and are the children of God, being the children of the resurrection. | For neither can they die any more : for they are equal unto the angels, and are sons of God, being sons of the resurrection. |

There are two remarkable passages in the Sermon on the Mount in which Christ applies the name given to himself in a peculiar sense in the fourth Gospel and in Paul's Epistles, to those who desired to be 'imitators of God as beloved children' (Eph. v. 1, R.V.). In these passages also the Revisers very properly translate 'sons' in place of 'children.'

### MATT. v. 9.

| | |
|---|---|
| Blessed are the peacemakers; for they shall be called the children of God. | Blessed are the peacemakers; for they shall be called sons of God. |

### MATT. v. 44, 45.

| | |
|---|---|
| Love your enemies . . . that ye may be the children of your Father which is in heaven. | Love your enemies . . . that ye may be sons of your Father which is in heaven. |

### LUKE vi. 35 (the parallel text).

| | |
|---|---|
| But love ye your enemies . . . and ye shall be the children of the Highest. | But love your enemies . . . and ye shall be sons of the Most High. |

This is the designation given to Jesus by the angel at the annunciation to his mother (Luke i. 32), 'He shall be great, and shall be called the Son of the Most High,' the Greek being the same, without the article 'the,' as is the case also in Matt. iv. 3, 'If thou art the Son of God,' literally 'a son.' Thus it will be seen that the title given to Jesus, as Mr. Sharpe remarks, 'is exactly the same as that given to all good men,' and in these instances by Jesus himself.

*Christ specially designated the Son of God.*

### ROM. i. 3.

| Authorized Version. | Revised Version. |
|---|---|
| Concerning his Son, Jesus Christ our Lord, which was made of the seed of David according to the flesh. | Concerning his Son, who was born of the seed of David according to the flesh. |

The same correction is made by the Revisers in Gal. iv. 4, where, instead of ' God sent forth his Son, made of a woman, made under the law,' they translate, ' born of a woman, born under the law.'    There has been much transcendental discussion on the employment in these cases of the term ' made,' as though it implied some mystic peculiarity in Christ's manner of birth.    The expression in the text just cited, ' born of a woman,' corresponds of course in meaning with the phrase Christ uses, Matt. xi. 11, 'Among them that are born of women;' and Bildad, Job xxv. 4, ' How can he be clean that is born of a woman ?'

The following alteration also is worthy of notice, in view of the supposed reference to Christ's superhuman nature :

### HEB. i. 4.

| Being made so much better than the angels. | Having become by so much better than the angels. |
|---|---|

---

### HEB. i. 1, 2.

| God who at sundry times, and in divers manners, spake in time past unto the Fathers by the Prophets, hath in these last days spoken unto us by *his* Son. | God, having of old time spoken unto the fathers in the prophets by divers portions and in divers manners, hath at the end of these days spoken unto us in *his* Son.* |
|---|---|
| | [* Gr. *a Son.* |

These corrections were anticipated in substance in the Improved Version, where also the contrast is made clear between the partial and varied revelations formerly given, and the complete and unique revealing in Christ. It is plain that the writer of the Epistle did not imagine that it was really the Second Person of the Trinity who had so often been described as having appeared already to the fathers in what have been called the 'theophanies' of the Old Testament. He had evidently no conception of God's having communicated with the Fathers in person, and the margin further suggests that he was intending to emphasize the fact of God's speaking now through a Son, not as formerly through inferior messengers. So far, indeed, was he from supposing any previous appearance of the Son upon earth, that he proceeds to describe the process of suffering by which as a Son he became himself perfected, having been heard by the Father in his prayers on account of 'his godly fear'—

### HEB. v. 7—9.

*Authorized Version.*

Who in the days of his flesh, when he had offered up prayers and supplications, with strong crying and tears, unto him that was able to save him from death, and was heard, in that he feared.* Though he were a Son, yet learned he obedience by the things which he suffered: and being made perfect, he became the author of eternal salvation unto all them that obey him.

[* Or, *for his piety.*

*Revised Version.*

Who in the days of his flesh, having offered up prayers and supplications, with strong crying and tears, unto him that was able to save him from* death, and having been heard for his godly fear, though he was a Son, yet learned obedience by the things which he suffered; and having been made perfect, he became unto all them that obey him the author† of eternal salvation.

[* Or, *out of.*    † Gr. *cause.*

### JOHN i. 14.

And we beheld his glory, the glory as of the only begotten of the Father.

And we beheld his glory, glory as of the* only begotten from the Father.

[* Or, *an only begotten from a Father.*

The alternative translation given in the note is the more important, that this title is given to Christ by no other writer of the New Testament, and it is one that he has nowhere himself claimed. It is doubtful whether the passage in John iii. 16—21 should be considered as John's report of what Christ said, or his own comment. In either case, the expression, 'God . . . gave his only begotten Son,' clearly grounds upon the present text. In Heb. i. 6 'the first-begotten' of the Authorized Version now reads 'the firstborn.'

But with whatever special meaning the title 'begotten of God' is applied to Christ, it should be noted that the expression is used also of his disciples. In 1 John v. 1, the Revisers translate, 'Whosoever believeth that Jesus is the Christ is begotten of God,' and 1 John ii. 29, 'Every one also that doeth righteousness is begotten of him.'

---

### Christ the Servant of God.

#### ACTS iv. 25—27, 29, 30.

| *Authorized Version.* | *Revised Version.* |
|---|---|
| Who by the mouth of thy servant David hast said . . . . and the rulers were gathered together against the Lord, and against his Christ. For of a truth against thy holy child Jesus, whom thou hast anointed, both Herod, &c. . . . and grant unto thy servants . . . that signs and wonders may be done by the name of thy holy child Jesus. | Who* by the Holy Ghost *by* the mouth of our father David thy servant didst say . . . . and the rulers were gathered together against the Lord, and against his Anointed.† For of a truth in this city against thy holy servant Jesus, whom thou didst anoint, both Herod, &c. . . . . and grant unto thy servants‡ . . . and that signs and wonders may be done through the name of thy holy Servant Jesus. |

[* The Greek text in this clause is somewhat uncertain.
† Gr. *Christ.*   ‡ Gr. *bondservants.*

So the Improved Version translated, 'against his anointed,' as the expression appears in the Psalm (ii. 2) here quoted, and 'through the name,' not 'by.' It has also 'thy holy servant Jesus,' justifying this rendering by pointing out the fact that the original word is the same as the term used just before of David. The same expression occurs in the speech of Peter (Acts iii. 13), 'The God of our fathers hath glorified his servant Jesus,' where the Revisers, while adding in the margin, 'or, *child*,' refer in explanation to the quotation from Isaiah in Matthew (xii. 18), 'Behold my servant whom I have chosen.' The remaining passage in which the word occurs has the same important variation, which will be found also in the Improved Version. Mr. Sharpe remarks that "the Greek word which originally meant 'child,' as son or daughter, is in the New Testament always used, like our 'boy' or 'lad,' to mean a servant, as at all times titles of youth have been used for persons of inferior rank."

### ACTS iii. 26.

| *Authorized Version.* | *Revised Version.* |
|---|---|
| Unto you first, God, having raised up his Son Jesus, sent him to bless you. | Unto you first, God, having raised up his Servant, sent him to bless you. |

The usual term of address to Jesus, 'Teacher,' the Revisers have put in the margin, leaving the old and less fitting word 'Master' in the text. This occurs even in John i. 38, where the better word is plainly suggested. But they have made an important correction in passages like the following—

### ACTS v. 42.

| And daily in the temple and in every house, they ceased not to teach and preach Jesus Christ. | And every day in the temple and at home, they ceased not to teach and to preach Jesus as the Christ. |
|---|---|

## SHEOL, HADES, HELL.

The American Company of Revisers of the Old Testament put on record upon the subject of this section some important corrections recommended by them, but which have not been made in the Revised Version.

For example, at Gen. xxxvii. 35, 'I will go down into the grave,' the marginal note explains, 'Heb. Sheol, the name of the abode of the dead, answering to the Greek Hades, Acts ii. 27.' But the New Version varies in its usage, sometimes translating the word, sometimes not. The Americans say, 'Substitute Sheol, wherever it occurs in the Hebrew text, for the renderings 'the grave,' 'the pit,' and 'hell.'

The word 'hell' is employed in the Authorized Version five times in three passages in Ezekiel and Isaiah, and is retained by the Revisers, with the addition of a sixth of their own, though in each case with the marginal notice that the Hebrew word is 'Sheol.' The passages are very striking ones. They relate to kingdoms and princes, predicting the ruin of their greatness, and the forms of imagery adopted throw considerable light upon the ideas of the Jewish people concerning the state of the dead. Speaking of the Assyrian power, the prophet Ezekiel (xxxi. 15) uses the expression, 'In the day when he went down to the grave,' which in the New Version reads, 'In the day when he went down to hell' (marg. 'Heb. *Sheol*'), an expression probably introduced with the view of bringing the text into accordance with the verse following: 'I made the nations to shake at the sound of his fall, when I cast him down to hell (marg. 'Heb. *Sheol*') with them that descend into the pit: and all the trees of Eden, the choice and best of Lebanon, all that drink water [the princes whom he had subdued], were comforted in the nether parts of the earth. They also went down into hell (marg. 'Heb. *Sheol*') with him unto them that be slain by the sword;

yea, they that were his arm, &c.' Mr. J. Scott Porter has in
each case 'the grave,' following the example of Archbishop
Newcome ; Dr. Noyes also translates 'the grave.' Dr. Cox[1]
would have preferred the uniform use of the term ' Hades' in
the Old as well as in the New Testament.    But the Hebrew
word might as readily become naturalized if always given in
its proper place.

In the following prophecy against Pharaoh (Ezek. xxxii. 18),
the several powers that had passed away are described as
lying in their places as in an Egyptian tomb, ready to hail
his fall to their own condition (*v.* 21): 'The strong among
the mighty[2] shall speak to him out of the midst of hell (marg.
' Heb. *Sheol'*) with them that help him.' So *v.* 27, 'And they
shall not lie with the mighty that are fallen of the uncircum-
cised, which are gone down to hell (marg. ' Heb. *Sheol'*) with
their weapons of war, and have laid their swords under their
heads.' The expression in *v.* 30 is, ' with them that go down
to the pit,' which is the word used by Mr. J. Scott Porter.

But the finest of these passages of prophetic imagery is in
Isaiah (chap. xiv.), the earliest in point of time.    It is here
the prince of Babylon that is addressed in *v.* 9 : ' Hell (marg.
' Heb. *Sheol'*) from beneath is moved for thee to meet thee
at thy coming : it stirreth up the dead for thee' (marg. 'or,
*the shades'*).    So *v.* 11 : ' Thy pomp is brought down to the
grave ;' in the new Version, 'to hell' (marg. ' Heb. *Sheol'*).
Again (*vv.* 14, 15): 'Thou hast said, I will ascend above
the heights of the clouds ; I will be like the Most High.
Yet thou shalt be brought down to hell, to the sides of the
pit ;' in the new Version, ' to the uttermost parts of the pit,'

---

[1] ' Expositions,' Second Series, 1886, p. 111.

[2] It may be remarked here by the way, that the Hebrew words so
translated in this instance are almost exactly the same which occur in
Is. ix. 6, and which are there translated, ' The Mighty God,' the supposed
application being to Christ.    The Revisers give no hint in that place
that the words are elsewhere translated differently.

or, as in *v.* 19, 'that go down to the stones of the pit,' where those lie that have not received honourable burial. The Revised margin gives notice here also that the Hebrew word translated 'hell,' as in the old Version, is 'Sheol.' In the opening verse, Dr. Lowth translates, 'Hades from beneath,' which is the word employed by the New Testament Revisers to denote the underworld, the state of the dead.

False confidence in presence of threatening dangers is forcibly expressed in a passage in Is. xxviii. 15. The Revisers do not change the word 'hell,' but only indicate in the margin that the original term is 'Sheol.' 'Because ye have said, We have made a covenant with death, and with hell are we at agreement; when the overflowing scourge shall pass through, it shall not come unto us.' Mr. Wellbeloved has, 'and with the grave made a league,' and Dr. Noyes, 'with the underworld.' The Revisers say also in *v.* 18, 'Your covenant with death shall be disannulled, and your agreement with hell shall not stand' (marg. 'Heb. *Sheol*'). Though the word 'hell' is retained, the margin shows that the use which has sometimes been made of these verses, as though they applied to defenders of wickedness and wrong as being in league with Satan, is not in harmony with the sense in which the prophet was speaking.

In another passage of simply local significance, the Revisers retain the word 'hell,' while noting that the Hebrew word is 'Sheol.' The prophet is reproaching the people with courting foreign alliances instead of serving and trusting the God of Israel. 'And didst send thine ambassadors far off, and didst debase thyself even unto hell' (Is. lvii. 9).

---

In the three following instances, the Revisers make the correction which the American Company would have introduced without the exceptions above noted. In all these cases the common idea of hell as a place of punishment was clearly

I

not in the mind of the writers. In many such passages the word formerly translated 'hell' is used as a mere term of comparison—

PROV. XV. 11.

| *Authorized Version.* | *Revised Version.* |
|---|---|
| Hell and destruction are before the LORD, how much more then the hearts of the children of men. | Sheol* and Abaddon† are before the LORD, how much more then the hearts of the children of men. |
| | [* Or, *the grave.*    † Or, *Destruction.* |

The alternative 'the grave' was adopted by Mr. Wellbeloved, as also in the similar passage that follows; Dr. Noyes has in both, 'the underworld':

JOB xxvi. 6.

| Hell is naked before him, and destruction hath no covering. | Sheol* is naked before him, and Abaddon† hath no covering. |
|---|---|
| | [* Or, *the grave.*    † Or, *Destruction.* |

PROV. xxvii. 20.

| Hell and destruction are never full; so the eyes of man are never satisfied. | Sheol and Abaddon are never satisfied; and the eyes of man are never satisfied. |
|---|---|

This allusion to the grave as 'swallowing up' all life without pause or satiety, is again made, in Habak. ii. 5, a term of comparison in reference to a man of grasping ambition, 'who enlargeth his desire as hell, and is as death, and cannot be satisfied.' The Revisers mention that the Hebrew word is 'Sheol,' but do not say why the term 'hell' is there left in the text. Mr. Wellbeloved translates the passage, 'who enlargeth his desire as the grave, and as death, and is not satisfied.'

In Is. v. 14 also the Revisers make no change, though they put in the margin, 'or, *the grave,* Heb. *Sheol.*' The prevailing idea of death is the same as in the passages just given. 'Therefore hell hath enlarged her desire, and opened her mouth without measure, and their glory and their multitude and their pomp, and he that rejoiceth among them, descend into it.'

In three passages which the Revisers have corrected, the term Sheol is employed to indicate an immeasurable extreme.

### DEUT. xxxii. 22.

| *Authorized Version.* | *Revised Version.* |
|---|---|
| For a fire is kindled in mine anger, and shall burn unto the lowest hell. | For a fire is kindled in mine anger, and burneth unto the lowest pit. |

'Or,' says the margin, 'in the Heb. *Sheol.*' Still better perhaps was Mr. Wellbeloved's translation, 'shall burn to the lowest depths,' that is to say—of the earth, where the abode of departed souls was believed to be.

In the following passage is set forth the unsearchable mystery of the Divine Nature, and the comparison is with the largest measures then conceivable: 'It is longer than the earth and broader than the sea'—

### JOB xi. 8.

| It is as high as heaven, what canst thou do? deeper than hell, what canst thou know? | *It is high as heaven, what canst thou do? deeper than Sheol,† what canst thou know? |
|---|---|
| | [* Heb. *The heights of heaven.* † Or, *the grave.* |

A kindred train of conception occurs in a well-known Psalm, in which Mr. Wellbeloved translates the word 'Sheol' 'the lower world:'

### Ps. cxxxix. 8.

| If I ascend up into heaven, thou art there: if I make my bed in hell, behold thou *art there.* | If I ascend up into heaven, thou art there: if I make my bed in Sheol, behold thou art there. |
|---|---|

The same contrast appears in Amos ix. 2, where, however, the Revisers have left the 'hell' of the Authorized Version, stating in the margin that the Hebrew word is 'Sheol.' 'There shall not one of them escape.  Though they dig into hell, thence shall my hand take them ; and though they climb up to heaven, thence will I bring them down.'  Mr. Wellbeloved's translation reads, 'Though they dig down to the lowermost world.'

---

The following amendment helps to make more clear what was the Hebrew conception of the underworld.  It will be observed how the use of the word 'grave' takes the point out of the passage :

### JOB xiv. 13.

| *Authorized Version.* | *Revised Version.* |
|---|---|
| O that thou wouldest hide me in the grave, that thou wouldest keep me in secret, until thy wrath be past. | Oh that thou wouldest hide me in Sheol,* that thou wouldest keep me secret, until thy wrath be past.<br><br>[* Or, *the grave.* |

In the nine passages following, the Revisers have very properly changed the word 'hell' of the Authorized Version :

### Ps. ix. 17.

| | |
|---|---|
| The wicked shall be turned into hell, and all the nations that forget God. | The wicked shall return to Sheol, even all the nations that forget God. |

Mr. Wellbeloved translates this, 'The wicked shall be turned into the lowermost world, all the nations that forget God.'  Compare with this the Revised Version of Ps. xxxi. 17, 'Let the wicked be ashamed, let them be silent in Sheol.' The following is a passage of similar purport—

## Ps. lv. 15.

| *Authorized Version.* | *Revised Version.* |
|---|---|
| Let death seize upon them, and let them go down quick into hell. | Let* death come suddenly upon them, let them go down alive into the pit.† |
| | [* Or, as otherwise read, *Desolations be upon them!*  † Heb. *Sheol.* |

## PROV. v. 5.

| Her feet go down to death, her steps take hold on hell. | Her feet go down to death, her steps take hold on Sheol.* |
|---|---|
| | [* Or, *the grave.* |

## PROV. vii. 27.

| Her house is the way to hell, going down to the chambers of death. | Her house is the way to Sheol,* going down to the chambers of death. |
|---|---|
| | [* Or, *the grave.* |

## PROV. ix. 18.

| But he knoweth not that the dead are there; and that her guests are in the depths of hell. | But he knoweth not that the dead* are there; that her guests are in the depths of Sheol. |
|---|---|
| | [* Or, *the shades*, Heb. *Rephaim.* |

## PROV. xv. 24.

| The way of life is above to the wise, that he may depart from hell beneath. | To the wise the way of life goeth upward, that he may depart from Sheol* beneath. |
|---|---|
| | [* Or, *the grave.* |

## PROV. xxiii. 14.

| Thou shalt beat him with the rod, and shalt deliver his soul from hell. | Thou shalt beat him with the rod, and shalt deliver his soul from Sheol.* |
|---|---|
| | [* Or, *the grave.* |

Mr. Wellbeloved translates here, 'the grave.' Either alternative word shows that the meaning is to deliver, not from punishment in the after life, but from an untimely end of this life. The same would appear to be the use and force of the word in the four preceding passages also.

---

Afflictions so extreme as to bring the sufferers to the point of death are frequently described in the Hebrew writings, but certainly with no idea of penal torments to follow.

### 2 SAM. xxii. 6, and Ps. xviii. 5.

| *Authorized Version.* | *Revised Version.* |
|---|---|
| The sorrows of hell compassed me about, the snares of death prevented me. | The cords of Sheol* were round about me, the snares of death came upon me. |
| | [* See Gen. xxxvii. 35 (where the use of the word is explained). |

Dr. G. V. Smith translates, 'The toils of the grave surrounded me, the snares of death surprised me;' and Mr. Wellbeloved has, in the second clause of the text in the Psalm, 'were spread before me.'

The same ideas occur in another Psalm, in which Mr. Wellbeloved renders, 'The toils of death surrounded me, and the distresses of the grave had found me.'

### Ps. cxvi. 3.

| The sorrows of death compassed me, and the pains of hell gat hold upon me.* | The cords of death compassed me, and the pains of Sheol* gat hold upon me. |
|---|---|
| [* Heb. *found me.* | [* Or, *the grave.* |

---

The allusion to the story of Jonah in Matt. xii. 40, which at least exhibits the popular idea of the time as to the underworld, though not probably the real interpretation of Christ's 'sign of Jonah the prophet' (for which see Luke xi. 30, 32), is made clearer by reference to the psalm of deliverance, which, coming before the 10th verse of chapter ii. of the book, is obviously misplaced. In Jon. ii. 2 the Revisers make no change : 'Out of the belly of hell cried I ;' but they indicate in the margin that 'hell' is in the Hebrew 'Sheol.'

---

### Ps. xvi. 9, 10.

| *Authorized Version.* | *Revised Version.* |
|---|---|
| My flesh also shall rest in hope. For thou wilt not leave my soul in hell, neither wilt thou suffer thine Holy One to see corruption. | My flesh also shall dwell in safety.* For thou wilt not leave my soul to Sheol, neither wilt thou suffer thine holy one† to see corruption.‡ |

[* Or, *confidently.* † Or, *godly; or, beloved.* ‡ Or, *the pit.*

Mr. Wellbeloved has, 'For thou wilt not abandon my soul to the lowermost world, nor suffer thy pious one to see corruption.' See this quoted in Peter's discourse at Pentecost (Acts ii. 27), which the Revised Version translates, 'Because thou wilt not leave my soul in Hades, neither wilt thou give thy Holy One to see corruption.' The Improved Version also had, 'Thou wilt not leave me in the grave.' The Apostle clearly understood the Psalm in this sense, but the Old Testament Revisers have kept nearer to the original in translating 'to,' not 'in.' The true sense, moreover, of the word translated corruption is not 'putrefaction,' as in Peter's argument. It is 'the pit,' as given here in the margin. See also, again, further on :

### ACTS ii. 31.

| | |
|---|---|
| Spake of the resurrection of Christ, that his soul was not left in hell, neither his flesh did see corruption. | Spake of the resurrection of the Christ, that neither was he left in Hades, nor did his flesh see corruption. |

The singular assertion in the Apostles' Creed, 'He descended into hell,' which was added, says Bishop Pearson, some time in the fourth century A.D., was chiefly grounded on this text. But it is a remarkable fact that in the psalm the writer is expressing the trust that his mortal life will be prolonged, not that his soul shall be restored to life after death. There are many passages in the Psalms to the same purport.

_____

All the passages in the Old Testament (15) in which the word 'hell' is retained in the New Version having been noticed, and some of the other texts (38) in which a useful and interesting change has been made, it remains to observe the treatment of the word adopted by the Revisers of the New Testament, taking first the places (13) where the term is still to be found, and which reflect for the most part the doctrine of the sect of Pharisees (see Jos. Antiq. xviii. 1, 3) respecting the state of the dead—

### MATT. xxiii. 15.

| *Authorized Version.* | *Revised Version.* |
|---|---|
| Ye make him twofold more the child of hell than yourselves. | Ye make him twofold more a son of hell* than yourselves.<br><br>[* Gr. *Gehenna*. |

'A son of hell' has the same meaning as 'the son of perdition' in John xvii. 12, not one predestinated to this end, but of a character deserving it; a base, worthless person; in Old Testament phrase 'a son of Belial.' See 1 Sam. xxv. 17 (R.V. margin). See also 1 Sam. xx. 31 and 2 Sam. xii. 5. In the first of these passages, although the New Version translates, with the Authorized, 'he shall surely die,' the note is subjoined, 'or, *is worthy to die*, Heb. *is a son of death*.' In the second, the new translation is given in the text, with the note, 'Heb. *a son of death*.'

### MATT. v. 22.[1]

| | |
|---|---|
| Shall be in danger of hell fire. | Shall be in danger of* the hell of fire.†<br><br>[* Gr. *unto* or *into*.     † Gr. *Gehenna of fire*. |

_____

[1] Dr. G. Vance Smith remarks here ('Texts and Margins,' p. 11) that Gehenna means etymologically 'Valley of Hinnom,' and he refers

## MATT. v. 29.

| *Authorized Version.* | *Revised Version.* |
|---|---|
| And not that thy whole body should be cast into hell. (So *v.* 30.) | And not thy whole body be cast into hell;* (and *v.* 30, 'go into hell.*) |
| | [* Gr. *Gehenna*. |

## MATT. xviii. 9.

| | |
|---|---|
| Rather than having two eyes to be cast into hell fire. | Rather than having two eyes to be cast into the hell of fire.* |
| | [* Gr. *Gehenna of fire*. |

## MARK ix. 43.

| | |
|---|---|
| Than having two hands, to go into hell, into the fire that never shall be quenched. | Than having thy two hands to go into hell,* into the unquenchable fire. |
| | [* Gr. *Gehenna*. |

This is repeated in *v.* 45, 'having two feet,' and *v.* 47, 'having two eyes.' Verses 44 and 46, which repeat the expression in *v.* 48, 'where their worm dieth not, and the fire is not quenched,' 'are omitted,' says the margin, 'by the best ancient authorities.' These two verses are therefore dropped out of the Bible.

## MATT. x. 28.

| | |
|---|---|
| But rather fear him which is able to destroy both soul and body in hell. | But rather fear him which is able to destroy both soul and body in hell.* |
| | [* Gr. *Gehenna*. |

---

to 2 Kings xxiii. 10, in explanation of the later use of the place for the burning of the refuse of Jerusalem. He rightly pleads that the word should have been inserted as a proper name in the text, and at the same time suggests that 'of fire' was probably a Hebraism for 'fiery' or 'burning.' 'The hell of fire' is perhaps an improvement on 'hell fire,' but the term Gehenna does not mean hell, although it was understood symbolically by the Jewish people to represent what is called in Matt. xxv. 41, 'the eternal fire which is prepared for the devil and his angels' (R. V.).

## LUKE xii. 5.

| *Authorized Version.* | *Revised Version.* |
| --- | --- |
| Fear him, which after he hath killed, hath power to cast into hell. | Fear him, which after he hath killed, hath power* to cast into hell.† |
| | [* Or, *authority.* † Gr. *Gehenna.* |

## JAMES iii. 6.

| The tongue is a fire . . . . it defileth the whole body, and setteth on fire the course of nature, and it is set on fire of hell. | The tongue is a fire . . . . which defileth the whole body, and setteth on fire the wheel of nature,* and is set on fire by hell. |
| --- | --- |
| | [* Or, *birth.* |

The Greek is 'Gehenna,' as in the other passages cited, though this note is not appended here, obviously through an oversight.

## 2 PET. ii. 4.

| For if God spared not the angels that sinned, but cast them down to hell, and delivered them into chains of darkness, to be reserved unto judgment. | For if God spared not angels when they sinned, but cast* them down to hell,† and committed them to pits‡ of darkness, to be reserved unto judgment. |
| --- | --- |
| | [* Or, *cast them into dungeons.* † Gr. *Tartarus.* ‡ Some ancient authorities read, *chains.* |

In the following passages the Authorized word 'hell' was used to translate quite a different term. The Revisers very properly indicate the distinction by giving the original word in the text—

## LUKE xvi. 23.

| And in hell he lift up his eyes, being in torments. | And in Hades he lifted up his eyes, being in torments. |
| --- | --- |

The Improved Version had here 'the Unseen State.' This is not to be confounded with Gehenna. The Greek idea of Hades, which from this parable it may be inferred that the Jewish people of Christ's time also entertained, distinguished between the two states in Hades, of Elysium and Tartarus, both in the same abode of Shades, but separated by a great gulf from each other. The expression, 'into Abraham's bosom,' used before of Lazarus, may remind the reader of the similar phrase in Matt. viii. 11, 'shall sit down with Abraham in the kingdom of God.'

## MATT. xvi. 18.

| *Authorized Version.* | *Revised Version.* |
|---|---|
| Upon this rock I will build my Church: and the gates of hell shall not prevail against it. | Upon this rock I will build my church; and the gates of Hades shall not prevail against it. |

The Improved Version translates here 'the gates of death.' It is no doubt a periphrasis for death, the idea intended to be conveyed being that the church should endure for generations to come. The expression may be found in Old Testament form in Is. xxxviii. 10, 'I shall go into the gates of the grave' (Heb. *Sheol*, R.V.).

## MATT. xi. 23.

| | |
|---|---|
| And thou, Capernaum, which art exalted unto heaven, shalt be brought down to hell. | And thou, Capernaum, shalt thou be exalted unto heaven? thou shalt go down * unto Hades. |
| | [* Many ancient authorities read, *be brought down.* |

In Luke x. 15, the corresponding passage, the reading of this note is adopted, instead of the Authorized 'be thrust down.' The contrast is obviously between the highest and the lowest points conceivable to the mind of the time, that is to say, the heavens above and the Sheol of the Old Testament below. The reader may be reminded of the text before cited from Ps. ix. (see p. 116).

---

In the two following passages, Hades is clearly the temporary place of departed spirits :

### REV. i. 18.

| *Authorized Version.* | *Revised Version.* |
|---|---|
| And have the keys of hell and of death. | And I have the keys of death and of Hades. |

### REV. xx. 13, 14.

| | |
|---|---|
| And death and hell* delivered up the dead which were in them, and they were judged every man according to their works. And death and hell were cast into the lake of fire : this is the second death.<br><br>  [* Or, *grave.* | And death and Hades gave up the dead which were in them, and they were judged every man according to their works. And death and Hades were cast into the lake of fire. This is the second death, *even* the lake of fire. |

---

The bottomless pit has been commonly supposed to be hell : the following passages will show the use of the word in the New Testament.

### REV. ix. 1.

| | |
|---|---|
| The key of the bottomless pit. | The key of the pit of the abyss. |

But the term 'abyss,' which the Authorized Version translated here 'bottomless pit,' is employed on two other occasions, one in Luke viii. 31, 'And they (the demons) intreated him that he would not command them to depart into the abyss' (A.V. 'into the deep'). The other text is—

## ROM. x. 7.

| *Authorized Version.* | *Revised Version.* |
|---|---|
| Who shall descend into the deep ? (that is, to bring up Christ again from the dead). | Who shall descend into the abyss? (that is, to bring Christ up from the dead). |

Abyss means bottomless, but there was no reason for translating the term 'bottomless pit' in either of these passages excepting the first, the one in which the Revised Version gives the more precise expression.

## REV. xvii. 8.

| The beast that thou sawest was, and is not, and shall ascend out of the bottomless pit, and go into perdition. | The beast that thou sawest was, and is not, and is about to come up out of the abyss, and to go* into perdition. |
|---|---|
| | [* Some ancient authorities read, *and he goeth.* |

## REV. xx. 1—3.

| And I saw an angel come down from heaven, having the key of the bottomless pit, and a great chain in his hand. And he laid hold on the dragon, that old serpent, which is the devil and Satan, and bound him a thousand years, and cast him into the bottomless pit, and shut him up, and set a seal upon him. | And I saw an angel coming down out of heaven, having the key of the abyss, and a great chain in* his hand. And he laid hold on the dragon, the old serpent, which is the Devil and Satan, and bound him for a thousand years, and cast him into the abyss, and shut it, and sealed it over him. |
|---|---|
| | [* Gr. *upon.* |

## THE WORDS DAMNED, DAMNABLE, DAMNATION.

The Revisers follow the Improved Version in 2 Pet. ii. 1, where, instead of 'damnable heresies,' they translate 'destructive heresies.' This was the only place in which the word 'damnable' occurred in the Old Version. The context shows how altogether unconnected these heresies were with mere differences of opinion, and how entirely their condemnation was justified upon moral, not intellectual, considerations. In the 3rd verse the Improved Version translated the term as it now appears in the Revised Version—

2 PET. ii. 3.

| *Authorized Version.* | *Revised Version.* |
|---|---|
| Whose judgment now of a long time lingereth not, and their damnation slumbereth not. | Whose sentence now from of old lingereth not, and their destruction slumbereth not. |

Several passages may be classed together which bear upon the question of future retribution. One of the strongest is the rebuke addressed to the Scribes for their hypocrisy, in Matt. xxiii. 33, which now reads, 'How shall ye escape the judgment of hell' (marg. 'Gr. *Gehenna*'), instead of the 'damnation of hell.' So reads also the Improved Version, 'the judgment of hell.'

Kindred with this is the denunciation against them, earlier in the same discourse (*v.* 14), in that they made long prayers to disguise wrongs done to widows. It is true that there is now no 14th verse in the chapter. It is inserted instead in the margin. But it appears in the text in the parallel places in Mark (xii. 40) and Luke (xx. 47), 'These shall receive greater condemnation,' the word used also in the Improved Version, instead of the old word 'damnation.'

In Mark iii. 29, the Improved Version translated, instead of the Authorized 'is in danger of eternal damnation,' 'is liable to everlasting punishment;' but the Revised Version reads, more literally, 'is guilty of an eternal sin.' The Improved Version has in the following text, 'condemnation;' the Revised translation is a still greater improvement :

### JOHN v. 29.

| *Authorized Version.* | *Revised Version.* |
|---|---|
| They that have done evil unto the resurrection of damnation. | They that have done * ill unto the resurrection of judgment. |
| | [* Or, *practised*. |

In the following passages the contexts show that the writers were not thinking of the eternal future which common usage connects so closely with the words 'damned,' 'damnation :'

### 1 TIM. v. 12.

| | |
|---|---|
| Having damnation, because they have cast off their first faith. | Having condemnation, because they have rejected their first faith. |

Or 'being blamable,' as the Improved Version perhaps too interpretatively rendered. It notes in the margin that Archbishop Newcome translated, 'having condemnation.' The passage refers to the proper treatment of young widows by the church, to save them from temptation.

In a text from Rom. xiii., political reformers were long supposed to be threatened with eternal perdition, as those who, in resisting the powers that be, resisted the ordinance of God. The Improved Version here anticipated the Revisers' correction :

### ROM. xiii. 2.

| | |
|---|---|
| And they that resist shall receive to themselves damnation. | And they that withstand shall receive to themselves judgment. |

It will be impossible for the fell associations which have long been connected with the terms 'damnation,' being 'damned,' 'damnable,' to survive the absolute disappearance of such words from the New Testament in the Revised Version. They were not to be found in the Old Testament, so that no change has there been needed ; but the new terms in the New Testament throw a discriminating light on the passages in which they occur, and of which it may be truly said, in several marked instances, that they now no longer exhibit the almost vindictive aspect of the older Version. It is perhaps needless to add that the Revisers have followed, in nearly every case of these required corrections, in the track of the Improved Version. The following passage is one most commonly quoted, though it occurs in the closing section of the Gospel which the Revisers mark off as doubtful, not being found, as they state in the margin, in 'the two oldest Greek manuscripts and some other ancient authorities.' The correction will be useful nevertheless—

### MARK xvi. 16.

| *Authorized Version.* | *Revised Version.* |
|---|---|
| He that believeth and is baptized shall be saved, but he that believeth not shall be damned. | He that believeth and is baptized shall be saved ; but he that disbelieveth shall be condemned. |

The following is a kindred passage in which the Improved Version translated 'condemned'—

### 2 THES. ii. 11, 12.

| | |
|---|---|
| And for this cause God shall send them strong delusion, that they should believe a lie : that they all might be damned who believed not the truth, but had pleasure in unrighteousness. | And for this cause God sendeth them a working of error, that they should believe a lie ; that they all might be judged who believed not the truth, but had pleasure in unrighteousness. |

In the three following instances the Improved Version and the Revised Version agree in the very proper use of the words 'condemn,' 'condemnation,' 'judgment'—

## Rom. iii. 8.

| *Authorized Version.* | *Revised Version.* |
|---|---|
| As some affirm that we say, Let us do evil, that good may come — whose damnation is just. | As some affirm that we say, Let us do evil, that good may come—whose condemnation is just. |

Evidently meaning, as Dean Alford says (who also translates 'condemnation'), that any such teaching would justly meet with 'the common detestation of all men.'

## Rom. xiv. 23.

| | |
|---|---|
| Happy is he that condemneth not himself in that thing which he alloweth. And he that doubteth is damned if he eat, because he eateth not of faith. | Happy is he that judgeth not himself in that which he approveth.* But he that doubteth is condemned if he eat, because he eateth not of faith. [* Or, *putteth to the test.* |

That a man is self-condemned if he acts in any doubtful matter without the full approval of his own conscience, is a statement worthy of the high Christian moralist, and the same principle practically applies in the case of those who would partake of sacred rites without their hearts' sympathy with the purport of them, and even in some cases with no due reflection upon their object. Such persons condemn their thoughtless action in the very act itself.

## 1 Cor. xi. 28, 29.

| | |
|---|---|
| But let a man examine himself, and so let him eat of that bread, and drink of that cup. For he that eateth and drinketh unworthily, eateth and drinketh damnation to himself, not discerning the Lord's body. | But let a man prove himself, and so let him eat of the bread, and drink of the cup. For he that eateth and drinketh, eateth and drinketh judgment unto himself, if he discern* not the body. [* Gr. *discriminate.* |

The Improved Version agreed with the note, 'not distinguishing the Lord's body.' The word 'unworthily,' which is now omitted as an interpolation, has long proved a terrible stumbling-block to many devout but timid believers.

K

## SATAN, DEVIL, EVIL ONE.

The personality and power of an evil spirit called the
Devil is so prominent an article of the common orthodox
belief, that it is of importance to note any corrections which
have been made in the Revised Version bearing upon this
subject.

One marked improvement which the American Revisers
suggested has unfortunately not been made in the Revised
text, though it is everywhere indicated in the margin. They
say, 'Substitute for 'devil' ('devils') the word 'demon'
('demons') wherever the latter word is given in the margin
(or represents the Greek words δαίμων, δαιμόνιον) ; and, for
'possessed with a devil' (or 'devils'), substitute either 'de-
moniac' or 'possessed with a demon' (or 'demons').'

Our Revisers leave the reader to find the true translation
in their notes. The large majority of the cases where this
correction is to be made relates to what we call demoniacs,
and it is well to notice that there is no such idea in the
New Testament as that of casting out 'devils :' it is always
'demons.' So in John x. 20, the Jews say of Jesus, 'He
hath a demon, and is mad ;' and in Matt. xi. 18, they said
of John the Baptist, 'He hath a demon.' In 1 Cor. x. 20, it
should be, as the margin indicates, 'they sacrifice to demons,'
a quotation from Deut. xxxii. 17, this being the word used
in the Septuagint (the Old Testament Revisers say 'demons'
in that passage, not 'devils'); and Rev. ix. 20, 'worship
demons.' In 1 Tim. iv. 1, the writer refers to doctrines not
'of devils,' but 'of demons ;' and in James ii. 19, it is not
said, 'the devils also believe and tremble,' but 'the demons.'
In Acts xvii. 18, the Athenians do not say of Paul that he

was a setter forth of strange gods, but of 'strange demons,' using the term in the Greek sense of supernatural beings.

The Old Testament Revisers have made this correction in another passage (Ps. cvi. 37) besides the one from Deut. xxxii. 17 above referred to. In two other places, Lev. xvii. 7 and 2 Chron. xi. 15, the 'devils' become 'he-goats,' or, as the margin notes, 'satyrs,' the same as are mentioned in Is. xiii. 21; probably objects of idolatrous worship.

With regard to the Devil, or Satan, the Prince of evil spirits, there is little in the Old Testament to suggest the existence of such a being. The word Satan is used in a few passages where the Old and the New Versions simply translate 'Adversary,' but it occurs as a proper name, with the article, only four times. The passages are here noted.

'Now there was a day when the sons of God came to present themselves before the LORD, and Satan came also among them' (Job i. 6). The margin explains the word Satan, 'that is, *the Adversary*.' It is explained in the same manner also in 1 Chron. xxi. 1, 'And Satan stood up against Israel, and moved David to number Israel.' In 2 Sam. xxiv. 1, this incident is described in a different way: 'The anger of the LORD was kindled against Israel, and he moved David against them to say, Go, number Israel and Judah.'

The same explanation is given also in Zech. iii. 1, where the Authorized Version reads, 'and Satan standing at his right hand to resist him,' the Revisers say, 'to be his adversary,' and note that the name means 'the Adversary.' The Septuagint translated the word by 'Diabolos,' an accuser or slanderer, as it did also in the following passage, one of the very few in the Old Testament in which the Spirit of Evil has been supposed to be referred to as a distinct personality:

## Ps. cix. 6.

| *Authorized Version.* | *Revised Version.* |
|---|---|
| Set thou a wicked man over him ; and let Satan stand at his right hand. | Set thou a wicked man over him ; and let an adversary* stand at his right hand. |
|  | [* Or, *Satan ;* or, *an accuser.* |

In the New Testament the common belief of the time in a Wicked Spirit, variously called Satan, the Devil, the Evil One, is clearly indicated in a considerable number of passages.   In one of these, however, the Revisers have made an interesting correction, which is not without importance in view of the almost omnipotent agency commonly attributed to the Devil—

## 2 TIM. ii. 26.

| And that they may recover themselves out of the snare of the devil, who are taken captive by him at his will. | And they may recover themselves* out of the snare of the devil, having been taken captive† by the Lord's servant unto the will of God.‡ |
|---|---|
|  | [* Gr. *return to soberness.*  † Gr. *taken alive.*    ‡ Or, *by the devil unto the will of God;* Gr. *by him, unto the will of him.*  In the Greek, the two pronouns are different. |

Whether the Revisers have really amended the Lord's Prayer (Matt. vi. 13) by changing 'deliver us from evil' into 'deliver us from the evil *one*,' is a point open to question. Mr. Gordon thinks[1] that by 'the evil one' the Devil was not necessarily intended, and observes that the titular capitals are not used.  But we learn from Dr. G. Vance Smith (*Texts*

[1] 'Christian Doctrine in the Light of New Testament Revision,' p. 42.

*and Margins,* p. 12) that the fact that the Greek Fathers took the word in the personal sense was the great reason for the revised rendering; and it should be noticed that the same change is made in the other prayer of Jesus, in John xvii. 15, which now reads, 'I pray not that thou shouldest take them from the world, but that thou shouldest keep them from the evil *one.*' So Matt. v. 37, 'Whatsoever is more than these is of the evil *one,*' where, however, the Revisers refer to another text of manifestly different import, which they translate, 'Resist not him that is evil.' But in all these passages they insert 'or, *evil*' in the margin, the Greek word being ambiguous, i.e. either masculine as denoting a person, or neuter as indicating evil in the abstract.

## WORLDS OR AGES. THE AGE TO COME. USE OF THE WORD ETERNAL.

In the New Testament the Authorized Version often has the term 'world' where the Revisers translate 'age,' either in their text or in the margin; the latter in about twenty places, the literal and probably more correct word thus appearing in the notes, not in the text. In only a few cases has the translation in the text been altered. One of these occurs in Hebrews (ix. 26). Instead of 'Once in the end of the world hath he appeared to put away sin by the sacrifice of himself,' we now read, 'at the end (marg. 'or, *consumma-tion*') of the ages hath he been manifested.' This was an obvious correction to make, since the world is now in its nineteenth Christian century, and the end is clearly not even yet. Probably for the same reason we now read, in 1 Cor. x. 11, 'they were written for our admonition, upon whom the ends of the ages are come,' not 'the ends of the world.'

In Heb. vi. 5, in place of 'have tasted the good word of

God and the powers of the world to come,' the Revisers introduce the exact translation into the text, 'the powers of the age to come,' as they have done also in Eph. iii. 9, where, instead of 'from the beginning of the world,' we now read, 'from all ages,' evidently with the object of assimilating the translation to that of Col. i. 26, where the original words are the same.

So in Eph. i. 21, Christ is exalted, after being raised from the dead, 'above every name that is named, not only in this world (marg. 'or, *age*'), but also in that which is to come.'

In one case the difference is important, as bearing on the authority and compass of what has been designated the mediatorial reign of Christ :

### MATT. xxviii. 20.

| *Authorized Version.* | *Revised Version.* |
|---|---|
| And lo, I am with you alway, even unto the end of the world. | And lo, I am with you alway,* even unto the end† of the world. |
| | [* Gr. *all the days.*    † Or, *the consummation of the age.* |

In relation to another important question, the same alternative rendering is given, viz. in Matt. xii. 32, where of a man speaking against the Holy Spirit, Christ says, 'It shall not be forgiven him, neither in this world (marg. 'or, *age*'), nor in that which is to come.'

It was probably to this age that should succeed to the Mosaic dispensation, what the Jews denominated the Age of the Messiah, that several passages like the following alluded :

### LUKE xx. 34, 35.

| | |
|---|---|
| The children of this world marry, and are given in marriage; but they which shall be accounted worthy to obtain that world, and the resurrection from the dead. | The sons of this world* marry, and are given in marriage ; but they that are accounted worthy to attain to that world,* and the resurrection from the dead. |
| | [* Or, *age.* |

Whatever theories may commend themselves to scientific speculation as to the ultimate destination of the material world, and whatever similar speculations may have been indulged or perhaps believed in by the Jewish people of the time of Christ, it is not certain, as may be learned from the Revisers' notes, that the end of the world as referred to in certain texts according to the Authorized translation should be understood in the material sense which that translation conveys. In three other passages, besides the one in Hebrews before referred to, though they retain the old version, the Revisers say in their notes, 'or, *consummation of the age.*' Thus where Christ says in the common version, 'The harvest is the end of the world' (Matt. xiii. 39, and so 40 and 49), this alternative is given in the margin; and in Matt. xxiv. 3 appears the same variation, so that the question of the disciples may have been, 'What shall be the sign of thy coming, and of the consummation of the age?' not 'the end of the world.'

In Mark x. 30, Jesus promises to the faithful disciple, in exchange for his loss of earthly relationships and advantages, compensations in this time, and in the world to come eternal life. The margin says, 'or, *in the age to come.*' This is again presented in the parallel passage in the third Gospel, with another correction which is also of importance—

### LUKE xviii. 30.

| *Authorized Version.* | *Revised Version.* |
|---|---|
| Who shall not receive manifold more in this present time, and in the world to come life everlasting. | Who shall not receive manifold more in this time, and in the world* to come eternal life.<br><br>[* Or, *age.* |

This change from 'everlasting' to 'eternal' is, and is obviously understood to be, of grave critical and moral importance. The Revisers carefully translate 'everlasting,' the

Greek word which has that proper meaning, even in a case like that of Rom. i. 20, where 'his everlasting power and divinity' certainly does not match in dignity of expression with the Authorized Version. But the other term derived from the word for 'age,' they prefer to render by another English word not necessarily implying endless duration, since it is often used in the Scriptures in connection with things naturally terminable and perishable, and in some cases only to contrast with temporary or temporal. Here are some examples of this correction, being about one-sixth of the whole in the New Testament. The first will remind the reader of the text from Luke just cited. It was a point in the Jewish doctrine of the coming age of the Messiah that there would then be a resurrection of the just, so that the pious of earlier times should not be left with this great 'promise of reward' unfulfilled. In the first passage Paul and Barnabas say, in addressing certain Jews who rejected the gospel they preached :—

### ACTS xiii. 46.

| *Authorized Version.* | *Revised Version.* |
|---|---|
| But seeing ye put it from you, and judge yourselves unworthy of everlasting life, lo, we turn to the Gentiles. | Seeing ye thrust it from you, and judge yourselves unworthy of eternal life, lo, we turn to the Gentiles. |

### 2 PET. i. 11.

| | |
|---|---|
| For so an entrance shall be ministered unto you abundantly into the everlasting kingdom of our Lord and Saviour Jesus Christ. | For thus shall be richly supplied unto you the entrance into the eternal kingdom of our Lord and Saviour Jesus Christ. |

### JOHN v. 24.

| | |
|---|---|
| He that heareth my word, and believeth on him that sent me, hath everlasting life, and shall not come into condemnation, but is passed from death unto life. | He that heareth my word, and believeth him that sent me, hath eternal life, and cometh not into judgment, but hath passed out of death into life. |

## John vi. 27.

| *Authorized Version.* | *Revised Version.* |
|---|---|
| Labour not for the meat which perisheth, but for that meat which endureth unto everlasting life. | Work not for the meat which perisheth, but for the meat which abideth unto eternal life. |

So in Rev. xiv. 6, we now read of an angel 'having an eternal gospel to proclaim,' instead of 'the everlasting gospel;' in Heb. xiii. 20, 'the blood of the eternal covenant,' not 'everlasting;' in 2 Thes. ii. 16, 'gave us eternal comfort and good hope through grace,' instead of 'everlasting comfort;' and in John xii. 50, 'I know that his commandment is life eternal.'

---

But the chief interest of this amendment in the Revised Version attaches naturally to the question of its bearing on the subject of retribution in the life to come. It is of special moment, therefore, to remark that the term 'everlasting' is no longer associated with the punishment of wicked men, whatever be otherwise the interpretation given to passages like those in Matt. xxv. 41, 'Depart from me, ye cursed (marg. 'or, *under a curse*'), into the eternal fire which is prepared for the devil and his angels;' and (*v.* 46) 'These shall go away into eternal punishment, but the righteous into eternal life.' There was no sufficient ground for the Authorized Version translating in this instance 'everlasting punishment,' the adjective in both clauses being the same.

It should be noticed here in connection with this description in Matthew of the coming of the Son of Man in glory and sitting on his throne of judgment, that in the next chapter the reader will find a statement which has been thought to justify the interpretation of this imagery in connection with the great events which shortly afterwards transpired in Palestine. It could hardly refer to a final judgment in some far distant future if Christ really said before the high-priest at his trial, not, as the Authorized Version represented, 'Here-after,' but, as the Revised Version says, 'Henceforth ye shall see the Son of Man sitting at the right hand of power, and coming on the clouds of heaven' (Matt. xxvi. 64). The same indication of a present date is given with perhaps even more marked emphasis in Luke xxii. 69, where the Revisers translate, 'From henceforth shall the Son of Man be seated at the right hand of the power of God.' It has been remarked as in keeping with the transcendental character of the Fourth Gospel that in a similar passage (John i. 51) the Revision shows that Jesus did not say, 'Hereafter ye shall see the heaven opened,' &c. The word 'hereafter' is now struck out.

---

In one instance where the Authorized Version has 'eternal life,' the Revision offers a striking and instructive change. The whole paragraph may be studied with advantage in its new form.

### 1 TIM. vi. 19.

| *Authorized Version.* | *Revised Version.* |
|---|---|
| That they may lay hold on eternal life. | That they may lay hold on the life which is *life* indeed. |

The Improved Version translated here 'the true life,' as also did Dean Alford. The Revisers' Version is at least more impressive, and seems to come nearer to the meaning of the original.

## PASSAGES BEARING ON THE QUESTION OF
## MAN'S FALLEN NATURE.

### GEN. viii. 21.

| *Authorized Version.* | *Revised Version.* |
|---|---|
| I will not again curse the ground any more for man's sake ; for the imagination of man's heart is evil from his youth. | I will not again curse the ground any more for man's sake, for* that the imagination of man's heart is evil from his youth. |
| | [* Or, *sake; for the.* |

The Old Version of this passage, which is now put in the margin, appeared to give a curious reason for the determination of the Almighty not again to curse the ground on account of human wickedness. The point of the statement there presented could only have been that the case was so hopeless that it was useless to try again the drastic remedy of which experiment had just been made. But how could this apply to Noah and his family, who were the only persons of the human race left, according to the story? The New Version makes the expression a simple reference to the reason for destroying the race which had been mentioned in Gen. vi. 5, implying that although Jehovah had punished men for this reason once, he would not again do so. The text may of course still be cited in proof of man's innate depravity, but the New Version clearly limits the application to the period before the Flood.

------

### Is. lxiv. 6.

| But we are all as an unclean thing, and all our righteousnesses are as filthy rags. | For we are all become as one that is unclean, and all our righteousnesses are as a polluted garment. |
|---|---|

The context shows that the prophet is describing a state
of things brought about by transgression, not one of inherent
depravity. The difference is well indicated in the correction,
' We are all become.'

In the context of the following passage also, it is shown
that the writer is describing a state of national feeling in
Israel at the particular period, and not the condition of
mankind universally.

JER. xvii. 9.

| *Authorized Version.* | *Revised Version.* |
|---|---|
| The heart is deceitful above all things, and desperately wicked: who can know it? | The heart is deceitful above all things, and it is desperately sick: who can know it? |

EPH. ii. 1.

| And you *hath he quickened* who were dead in trespasses and sins. | And you *did he quicken* when ye were dead through your trespasses and sins. |
|---|---|

The spiritual deadness had grown from deeds of wickedness, not from any hopeless depravity of nature. It is true
that immediately afterwards we find the statement, ' Ye were
by nature children of wrath even as the rest' (R.V.), the expression corresponding with the phrase in verse 2, 'sons of
disobedience;' but this phrase explains the other—' Being
disobedient, ye were obnoxious to the penalty of wrong-
doing.' Compare Gal. ii. 15, ' We being Jews by nature, and
not sinners of the Gentiles,' where the contrast does not bear
upon moral qualities, but upon the Jewish national assumption that the Gentile world was unclean, while they alone
were the consecrated people of God. A claim of the same
kind, probably following the line of this suggestion, was
made on behalf of the Christian community in 1 John v. 19,
' We know that we are of God, and the whole world lieth in
the evil one' (R.V.).

In a passage which will be again referred to, 2 Cor. v. 14 (p. 148), Paul speaks of all as dying in another sense, suggested by the peculiar view which he held of the effects of Christ's death as the second Adam, the representative of the race. If Christ died for all in this capacity, then in his death all died. (See the same important correction elsewhere, e.g. 'died with Christ,' not 'be dead with,' Rom. vi. 8.) This reads in the Authorized Version, 'then were all dead,' as though it had been thus demonstrated that mankind was universally under a curse and dead to everything pure and good—dead in sin, to use a theological phrase. The Apostle's argument is somewhat subtile, and not much after the mode of modern thinking, but the particular inference in question is not one of depreciation of man's nature, while it does most clearly justify the largest hope for humanity in regard to its final destiny.

---

### GAL. v. 17.

| *Authorized Version.* | *Revised Version.* |
|---|---|
| For the flesh lusteth against the Spirit, and the Spirit against the flesh : and these are contrary the one to the other : so that ye cannot do the things that ye would. | For the flesh lusteth against the Spirit, and the Spirit against the flesh : for these are contrary the one to the other : that ye may not do the things that ye would. |

So Dean Alford corrects. There is no hint of invincible moral impotence, as in the Authorized Version.

---

### PHIL. iii. 20, 21.

| | |
|---|---|
| For our conversation is in heaven, from whence also we look for the Saviour, the Lord | For our citizenship* is in heaven ; from whence also we wait for a Saviour, the Lord |
| | [* Or, *commonwealth*. |

| *Authorized Version.* | *Revised Version.* |
|---|---|
| Jesus Christ : who shall change our vile body, that it may be fashioned like unto his glorious body. | Jesus Christ : who shall fashion anew the body of our humiliation, that it may be conformed to the body of his glory. |

The writer had evidently in his mind the contrast which he had before remarked (Phil. ii. 7, 8, 9) between the prior lowly estate and the after glory of Christ. The same contrast was to be observed in the experience and hope of his followers, who are, says the Apostle, 'joint-heirs with Christ; if so be that we suffer with him that we may be also glorified with him' (Rom. viii. 17, R.V.). The idea is a very familiar one with Paul. The expression, 'our vile body,' has commonly been associated by preachers with the doctrine of man being under a curse in the very elements of his material and mortal constitution. The amendment is in this view a very striking one.

## REDEMPTION, ATONEMENT, FORGIVENESS.

In 1 Cor. i. 23 occurs a declaration which has been often made the text of sermons on the popular doctrine of the Atonement, showing its supreme importance in the explanation of the redeeming work of Christ. But when the Apostle says, 'We preach Christ crucified,' the context proves that he was not at the moment thinking of the legal or moral effect of Christ's death, but of the objections raised by Jews and Greeks to the fact itself that he had died, and as they thought died in infamy. The Revised margin suggests the real point of their difficulty. It would read, 'We preach a Messiah crucified.' This was what they found it hard to believe in, with their preconceptions respecting the Messiahship, or as to the means of elevating and redeeming mankind.

------

ROM. v. 11.

| *Authorized Version.* | *Revised Version.* |
|---|---|
| Our Lord Jesus Christ, by whom we have now received the atonement. | Our Lord Jesus Christ, through whom we have now received the reconciliation. |

The Improved Version translated in the same way. 'Very probably,' says Dr. G. Vance Smith (*Texts and Margins,* p. 30), 'the word Atonement was used by the translators of 1611 in the older sense of reconciliation.' It has now altogether disappeared in the Revised Version. Dr. Smith notices that the Revisers have not been true to the doctrine of salvation proceeding from the love of God, in the addition they make at verse 9, where the Authorized Version reads, 'We shall be saved from wrath.' They make this out to be the wrath of God. But the Apostle gives no idea of God being reconciled from a previous state of anger, though he might possibly have had in his mind 'the wrath to come' elsewhere referred to. There was no need for any addition to be made to 'the wrath' of the original.

Was this addition possibly suggested by the Authorized

text in Ps. vii. 11, which reads, 'God judgeth the righteous, and God is angry *with the wicked* every day,' but which the Old Testament Revisers translate, 'God is a righteous judge, yea a God that hath indignation every day,' simply emphasizing the stern element of justice, but not marking out this or that class of men as obnoxious to it?

---

### Eph. iv. 32.

| *Authorized Version.* | *Revised Version.* |
|---|---|
| Forgiving one another, even as God for Christ's sake hath forgiven you. | Forgiving each other, even as God also in Christ forgave you.* |
| | [* Many ancient authorities read, *us.* |

The idea of men being forgiven for Christ's sake, or through the merits of Christ, appears nowhere in the Revised Version. The Improved Version translated the passage, 'As God also through Christ hath forgiven you.'

### Col. iii. 13.

| Even as Christ forgave you, so also do ye. | Even as the Lord* forgave you, so also do ye. |
|---|---|
| | [* Many ancient authorities read, *Christ.* |

'So most of our oldest MSS.,' says Dean Alford, who, however, understands that the Lord means Christ, referring to the text above cited to explain that there 'the forgiveness is traced to its source God in Christ.' In either case it is God who forgives; and Christ could only forgive in God's name.

---

### Heb. ix. 22.

| And almost all things are by the law purged with blood: and without shedding of blood is no remission. | And according to the law, I may almost say, all things are cleansed with blood, and apart from shedding of blood there is no remission. |
|---|---|

The New Version brings out the fact more clearly that in the last clause the writer was not stating an abstract truth or principle in regard to the pardon of sin, as has been commonly supposed, but was rather indicating, and reasoning from, a well-known characteristic feature of the Jewish ceremonial law. The Improved Version also gave the correct sense, though not in so marked a manner.

### Rom. iii. 25.

| *Authorized Version.* | *Revised Version.* |
|---|---|
| Jesus Christ, whom God hath set forth* to be a propitiation, through faith in his blood. | Christ Jesus, whom God set forth * *to be* a propitiation,† through faith, by his blood.‡ |
| [* Or, *foreordained.* | [* Or, *purposed.* † Or, *to be propitiatory.* ‡ Or, *faith in his blood.* |

So that faith in the blood of Christ is another of the popular phrases for which it is seen there is no sufficient warrant in the New Testament. The phrase appears in no other passage, and here it is placed in the margin. Dean Alford remarks that 'such an expression as faith in the blood of Christ would be unexampled . . . besides, the clause ought to be, ' by his blood,' and so it now reads.'

### Rev. i. 5.

| | |
|---|---|
| Unto him that loved us, and washed us from our sins in his own blood. | Unto him that loveth us, and loosed* us from our sins by† his blood. |
| | [* Many authorities, some ancient, read, *washed.* † Gr. *in.* |

Compare with this the following—

### 1 Cor. vi. 11.

| | |
|---|---|
| And such were some of you; but ye are washed, but ye are sanctified, but ye are justified in the Name of the Lord Jesus, and by the Spirit of our God. | And such were some of you: but ye were washed,* but ye were sanctified, but ye were justified in the name of the Lord Jesus, and in the Spirit of our God. |
| | [* Gr. *washed yourselves.* |

L

## COL. i. 14.

| *Authorized Version.* | *Revised Version.* |
| --- | --- |
| In whom we have redemption through his blood, *even* the forgiveness of sins. | In whom we have our redemption, the forgiveness of our sins. |

In the corresponding passage in Ephesians (i. 7), the expression appears, which is now omitted here, 'In whom we have our redemption through his blood, the forgiveness of our trespasses' (R. V.).

---

## 1 PET. iv. 1.

| Forasmuch, then, as Christ suffered for us in the flesh. | Forasmuch, then, as Christ suffered in the flesh. |
| --- | --- |

The object of Christ's suffering is described elsewhere in the New Testament, but not here. A similar omission may be noted in two of the following passages, though the third does express the idea that Christ's was a self-sacrifice :

## 1 COR. v. 7.

| For *even* Christ, our Passover, is sacrificed for us. | For our Passover also hath been sacrificed, *even* Christ. |
| --- | --- |

## HEB. i. 3.

| When he had by himself purged our sins. | When he had made purification of sins. |
| --- | --- |

## HEB. ix. 26.

| But now once in the end of the world hath he appeared to put away sin by the sacrifice of himself. | But now once at the end* of the ages hath he been manifested to put away sin by the sacrifice of himself.† |
| --- | --- |
|  | [* Or, *consummation.*    † Or, *by his sacrifice.* |

Compare with these two passages one from Paul which may have suggested them. He says (Gal. i. 4), 'who gave himself for our sins, that he might deliver us out of this present evil world' (marg. 'or, *age*') ; that is, to bring in the purified state which would come with the age of the Messiah.

It is right to notice here that in Rom. viii. 3, where the Authorized Version reads, 'God sending his own Son in the likeness of sinful flesh, and for sin, condemned sin in the flesh,' the Revisers have inserted in the text, 'and as an offering for sin,' putting 'or, *for sin*,' in the margin. The American Revision Company object to this. They say, 'let the margin ('*and for sin*') and the text exchange places.' The Improved Version has 'on account of sin,' which is Dean Alford's explanation of the phrase.

---

The conviction that the martyr sufferings of a saintly man, or of an elect body of men such as constituted the true Israel of the Prophets, and whom Isaiah in particular designates the 'Servant of God,' might be understood to expiate the transgressions of their nation, was familiar to the Jewish people, as appears, for example, in Is. liii. 8 : 'For the transgression of my people was he stricken ;' where the margin reads, 'or to whom the stroke was due ;' the completion of the sentence thus depending on the preceding verb, 'he was cut off.' The fourth verse throws further light on this view : 'Surely he hath borne our griefs and carried our sorrows' (marg. 'Heb. *sicknesses*'). From this marginal variation may be understood the quotation of the verse in Matt. viii. 17, 'Himself took our infirmities, and bare our diseases' (R.V.), applied with reference to Christ's miracles of healing. But this quotation, though it illustrates the free manner in which the New Testament writers made use of the older writings, hardly bears upon the main idea of the chapter in Isaiah, the key to which may perhaps be found in verse 11, where the slight change from 'for' to 'and' is significant. Instead of 'by his knowledge shall my righteous servant justify many, for he shall bear their iniquities,' we now read, 'and he shall bear,' &c.  The margin also should be noted.  In place of 'shall justify many,' the alternative is given, 'or, *shall make many righteous.*'

---

### 2 COR. v. 14, 15.

| *Authorized Version.* | *Revised Version.* |
|---|---|
| For the love of Christ con-straineth us, because we thus judge: that if one died for all, then were all dead: and that he died for all, that they which live should not henceforth live unto themselves, but unto him which died for them, and rose again. | For the love of Christ con-straineth us; because we thus judge, that one died for all, therefore all died; and he died for all, that they which live should no longer live unto themselves, but unto him who for their sakes died and rose again. |

That Christ is represented in the New Testament, and especially in the Epistles, to have died in the interest of the whole family of man, has never been questioned by Unita-rians.  The New Version makes this point very distinct.  But of a penal death in substitution for the punishment of the race there is here no trace.  Christ died, not as a substitute for sinful men, but for their sakes, on their behalf.  The Revisers might have corrected the same ambiguity in the English in Rom. xiv. 15, 'Destroy not with thy meat him for whom Christ died,' since the Greek preposition is the same as the one here used, and with the same case, the proper meaning of which, as Unitarians have always insisted, is the meaning given here in the Revised Version.  Compare with this the following, where the Authorized Version is evidently amended for uniformity of rendering—

### PHIL. i. 29.

| For unto you it is given in the behalf of Christ, not only to believe on him, but also to suffer for his sake. | Because to you it hath been granted in the behalf of Christ, not only to believe on him, but also to suffer in his behalf. |

The following correction also deserves notice, because the Greek expresses the same view, 'in the interest of,' or 'on account of,' by the use of another preposition, but with no idea of a substitution having been made:

### 1 COR. viii. 11.

| *Authorized Version.* | *Revised Version.* |
|---|---|
| And through thy knowledge shall the weak brother perish, for whom Christ died. | For through* thy knowledge he that is weak perisheth, the brother for whose sake Christ died.<br><br>[* Gr. *in.* |

---

The idea of self-sacrifice for another's welfare has nothing in it of the substitutionary character implied in certain renderings of the Old Version. This is fairly brought out in the following passages, by the expression, 'giving oneself up for.' On the former of the two, Dean Alford explains 'gave himself up to death.' The Improved Version reads, 'delivered himself up.' In the second text it has the same expression as the Revisers employ—

### GAL. ii. 20.

| | |
|---|---|
| The life which I now live in the flesh, I live by the faith of the Son of God, who loved me, and gave himself for me. | That life which I now live in the flesh I live in faith, *the faith* which is in the Son of God, who loved me and gave himself up for me. |

### EPH. v. 25, 26.

| | |
|---|---|
| Even as Christ also loved the Church, and gave himself for it; that he might sanctify and cleanse it with the washing of water by the word. | Even as Christ also loved the Church, and gave himself up for it; that he might sanctify it, having cleansed it by the washing* of water with the word.<br><br>[* Gr. *laver.* |

## CONVERSION.

### Ps. xix. 7.

| *Authorized Version.* | *Revised Version.* |
|---|---|
| The law of the Lord is per-fect, converting* the soul. | The law of the Lord is per-fect, restoring the soul. |
| [* Or, *restoring.* | |

Mr. Wellbeloved translated 'refreshing the soul,' and Dr. Noyes 'reviving,' but Mr. S. Sharpe followed the old margin 'restoring,' which is adopted in the Revised text. There is nothing of 'conversion,' in the modern orthodox sense, in the passage as now read. Nor is it to be found in the following text, nor the accompanying conception of periods of 'Revival' when mystical conversions have been often supposed to occur in great numbers—

### ACTS iii. 19.

| Repent ye, therefore, and be converted, that your sins may be blotted out, when the times of refreshing shall come from the presence of the LORD. | Repent ye, therefore, and turn again, that your sins may be blotted out, that so there may come seasons of refreshing from the presence of the LORD. |
|---|---|

In Ps. li. 13, the expression is used, 'sinners shall be con-verted unto thee,' but with the marginal explanation, 'or, *return.*' Mr. Wellbeloved translates, 'shall turn themselves.' In Is. lx. 5 the correction is made in the text of the New Version, not the margin. Instead of 'the abundance of the sea shall be converted unto thee, the forces of the Gentiles shall come unto thee,' we now read, 'shall be turned unto thee, the wealth of the nations shall come unto thee.'

The term 'convert' occurs in one passage of the Old Testament, and it is retained in the Revised Version, 'Zion shall be redeemed with judgment, and her converts with righteousness' (Is. i. 27), where the old margin read, 'or, *they that return of her,*' which the Revisers also insert in the new margin. Mr. S. Sharpe translates, 'those that are brought back to her.' There is no allusion to converts in the ordinary theological sense.

The only other passage besides these in which the term is found in the Authorized Version of the Old Testament, is remarkable as having been four times quoted in the New Testament. In each case the word is so changed as to remove altogether the idea of the mystical process commonly associated with the term, as a term of hortatory theology—

### Is. vi. 10.

| *Authorized Version.* | *Revised Version.* |
|---|---|
| Make the heart of this people fat . . . lest they . . . understand with their heart, and convert, and be healed. | Make the heart of this people fat . . . lest they . . . understand* with their heart, and turn again, and be healed.<br><br>[* Or, *their heart should understand.* |

### MATT. xiii. 15.

| | |
|---|---|
| Lest at any time they should . . . understand with their heart, and should be converted, and I should heal them. | Lest haply they should . . . understand with their heart, and should turn again, and I should heal them. |

At the parallel place in Mark the same correction is made :

### MARK iv. 12.

| | |
|---|---|
| Lest at any time they should be converted, and their sins should be forgiven them. | Lest haply they should turn again, and it should be forgiven them. |

Luke introduces the reference into Christ's explanation of the parable (Luke viii. 12), 'Then cometh the devil and taketh away the word from their heart, that they may not believe and be saved' (R.V.). There are two other cases in which the prophecy is quoted—

### JOHN xii. 40.

| | |
|---|---|
| That they should not see with their eyes, nor understand with their heart, and be converted, and I should heal them. | Lest they should see with their eyes, and perceive with their heart, and should turn, and I should heal them. |

In the similar instance in Acts xxviii. 27, 'and should be converted' now reads, 'and should turn again.'

The 'conversion of the Gentiles' (Acts xv. 3) is naturally and properly retained, as it was also in the Improved Version. In James v. 19, the idea of one person inducing another to turn back 'from the error of his way' is present in the Old Version, which probably led the Revisers to think the change needless, so we still read, if 'one convert him,' 'he which converteth a sinner.' But in Luke the remarkable case is described of one who, having grievously 'erred from the truth' by denying Christ, did afterwards 'turn again,' or become 'converted.' Here the Revisers introduce the correction in the warning and exhortation to Peter:

### LUKE xxii. 32.

| *Authorized Version.* | *Revised Version.* |
|---|---|
| And when thou art converted, strengthen thy brethren. | And do thou, when once thou hast turned again, stablish thy brethren. |

This is an improvement upon the Improved Version, 'when thou hast returned,' though that phrase also was probably intended to express the same idea.

But the amendment which most strikingly exhibits the altered aspect of Scriptural expression in relation to the common doctrine and teaching of conversion, is made in the well-known and often-used text of Christ's lesson of humility to the disciples. This exhausts the collection of passages in which the word is employed:

### MATT. xviii. 3.

| Except ye be converted, and become as little children, ye shall not enter into the kingdom of heaven. | Except ye turn, and become as little children, ye shall in no wise enter into the kingdom of heaven. |

# ELECTION, JUSTIFICATION, SALVATION.

### ACTS ii. 47.

| *Authorized Version.* | *Revised Version.* |
|---|---|
| And the Lord added to the church daily such as should be saved. | And the Lord added* to them day by day those that were being saved. |
| | [* Gr. *together.* |

The idea of personal election is therefore no longer implied. The American Revisers would put 'those that were being saved' in the margin, and in the text, 'those that were saved,' which is the translation of the Improved Version.

They do not, however, hold to the change in the Revised Version of 'them that perish,' and 'us which are saved' (1 Cor. i. 18), to 'them that are perishing,' and 'us which are being saved.'   See also 2 Cor. ii. 15.

---

In the following passage the phrase, 'made us accepted in,' loses its character of exceptional favour, in the general grace bestowed upon men in Christ :

### EPH. i. 5, 6.

| Having predestinated us unto the adoption of children by Jesus Christ to himself, according to the good pleasure of his will: to the praise of the glory of his grace, wherein he hath made us accepted in the beloved. | Having fore-ordained us unto adoption as sons through Jesus Christ unto himself, according to the good pleasure of his will, to the praise of the glory of his grace, which* he freely bestowed on us in the Beloved. |
|---|---|
| | [* Or, *wherewith he endued us.* |

---

In Mal. iii. 17 the Authorized Version, 'And they shall be mine, saith the LORD of hosts, in that day when I make up my jewels,' has been thought to refer to the gathering in of the elect.   The Revised Version reads, 'they shall be mine in the day that I do make, even a peculiar treasure.' Dr. Noyes makes the sense much more clear, 'And they shall be to me in the day which I appoint, as my own possession.' All agree in what follows, 'And I will spare them as a man spareth his own son that serveth him.'

---

ROM. v. 18.

| *Authorized Version.* | *Revised Version.* |
|---|---|
| Therefore as by the offence of one *judgment* came upon all men to condemnation, even so by the righteousness of one *the free gift* came upon all men unto justification of life. | So then as through one trespass the *judgment came* unto all men to condemnation ; even so through one act of righteousness *the free gift came* unto all men to justification of life. |

So Dean Alford translates, 'through one trespass,' and 'one righteous act,' but instead of the words supplied which are put in italics he would read, 'the issue was,' in both cases. The Improved Version notes here the terms of universality employed, showing that the whole race, and not a chosen few, 'derived greater benefits from the mission of Christ than they suffered injury from the fall of Adam.'

---

In the next passage, peace with God does not now follow from the justification by faith, but rather the duty of seeking that peace is imposed with greater force, in consideration of the higher ground of privilege and hope which it is granted to believers to occupy :

ROM. v. 1, 2.

| | |
|---|---|
| Therefore being justified by faith, we have peace with God, through our Lord Jesus Christ. By whom also we have access by faith into this grace wherein we stand, and rejoice in hope of the glory of God. | Being therefore justified by faith, let us have peace with God through our Lord Jesus Christ; through whom also we have had our access by faith into this grace wherein we stand ; and let us rejoice in hope of the glory of God. |

Perhaps the best comment on this text may be found in the supreme value attributed to faith in the grace and truth of Christ : 'But as many as received him, to them gave he the right' (a suggestive change from the Authorized 'power') 'to become children of God, even to them that believe on his name' (John i. 12 ; see also p. 105). Men have learned in Christ and through Christian teaching their true relation to his and their Father.

---

HEB. x. 38.

| *Authorized Version.* | *Revised Version.* |
|---|---|
| Now the just shall live by faith : but if any man draw back, my soul shall have no pleasure in him. | But my righteous one* shall live by faith: and if he shrink back, my soul hath no pleasure in him. |
| | [* Some ancient authorities read, *the righteous one.* |

This is quoted from Habak. ii. 4, which reads, 'the just shall live by his faith,' ' or,' adds the Revised margin, '*in his faith-fulness,*' which is in entire keeping with the evident purport of the passage here, that the great end of salvation is only to be secured by steadfast faithfulness to the true way of salvation. The possibility of any of the elect saints falling from grace was inconceivable to the old translators. The final perseverance of the saints, the Calvinistic doctrine, was the common Protestant belief of the time.

It is to be noticed on this point that the Revised Version has in Gal. v. 4, 'Ye are fallen away from grace,' instead of 'fallen from ;' and in Heb. vi. 6, instead of 'if they shall fall away,' 'and then fell away.' Macknight says that Beza introduced the 'if,' that the text might not appear to contradict the doctrine of the perseverance of the saints.

---

JAMES ii. 14.

| *Authorized Version.* | *Revised Versson.* |
| --- | --- |
| What doth it profit, my brethren, though a man say he hath faith, and have not works? Can faith save him? | What doth it profit, my brethren, if a man say he hath faith, but have not works? Can that faith save him? |

It is interesting to observe in an early Christian writing a similar practical view of what constituted the state of salvation as understood by the first Christians. It is given to the bride of the Lamb (Rev. xix. 8) to array herself in fine linen, clean and white, which is then explained to mean the righteousness of saints. The New Version reads, 'in fine linen bright and pure; for the fine linen is the righteous acts of the saints.'

# THE FREE GRACE OF GOD.

### 2 COR. v. 11.

| *Authorized Version.* | *Revised Version.* |
|---|---|
| Knowing therefore the terror of the Lord, we persuade men. | Knowing therefore the fear of the Lord, we persuade men. |

That is, says Dean Alford, being God-fearing men, we are striving to convince men of our honesty of purpose ; not, as the Authorized Version seemed to say, that the Apostle was moved by the terribleness of God to urge men to repentance.

Indeed, the Jewish people had not the terror of the Lord which forms so conspicuous an element in the Calvinistic theology. Their sense of his merciful kindness appears everywhere in the ancient books. Even in the giving of the law of the Ten Commandments he is represented as contrasting his treatment of the disobedient and of the good, visiting the iniquities of the one to a few generations, but showing mercy to the other to the thousandth generation. The Revised Version of Ex. xx. 6 repeats the translation of the Authorized, 'showing mercy unto thousands of them that love me,' but exhibits the better sense in the margin ('or, *a thousand generations*'). As the Revisers refer for this to Deut. vii. 9, where the idea is very clearly expressed, it seems a pity that it was not inserted in the text.

A similar contrast of the great goodness of God with his acts of necessary judgment would seem indicated in Rom. vi. 23, 'the wages of sin is death, but the gift of God is eternal life,' which the Revision emphasizes by translating, 'the free gift of God.'

Ps. lxvii. 5.

| *Authorized Version.* | *Revised Version.* |
|---|---|
| Let the people praise thee, O God ; let all the people praise thee. | Let the peoples praise thee, O God; let all the peoples praise thee. |

The amendment here will be found also in Mr. Wellbeloved's Version. It accords with the whole tenour of the Psalm, which shows that the writer's thought embraced other nations besides his own. So in Is. lv. 4, the context indicates the accession of foreign nations to the worship of the God of Israel, where the prophet says of the expected leader, or prince, 'Behold, I have given him for a witness to the peoples, a leader and commander to the peoples' (R.V). Something of the same enlargement of view appears in Is. lvi. 7, 'Mine house shall be called a house of prayer for all peoples,' which is quoted in Mark xi. 17 with a correction restoring the text to the original form, reading, instead of 'called of all nations the house of prayer,' 'called a house of prayer for all the nations.'

A noticeable improvement is made by the similar correction in Mic. iv. 1, 3, 5 : 'And peoples shall flow unto it'—'And he shall judge between many peoples, and shall reprove strong nations afar off . . .'

It should, however, be noted that in Deut. xxxiii. 3 we find, instead of ' Yea, he loved the people,' ' Yea, he loveth the peoples' (M. ' or, *tribes*'), where only Israel can have been intended ; as also, perhaps, in Gen. xlix. 10.[1] But see Deut. xxxiii. 19, where possibly a wider extension of the term may be implied, as it certainly is in many other places.

---

The truly catholic conception of the Christian Church attributed to Jesus in the Fourth Gospel (x. 16) is admirably

[1] "' Peoples' for 'people,' here and often ; a small but important change," says Dr. Driver.—Expositor, third series, Vol. II. p. 7. 1885.

brought out in the Revised Version by the correction of a single word. Instead of 'there shall be one fold and one shepherd,' we now read, 'and they shall become one flock, one shepherd.'

---

### JOHN i. 9.

| *Authorized Version.* | *Revised Version.* |
|---|---|
| That was the true Light, which lighteth every man that cometh into the world. | There* was the true light, even *the light* which lighteth every† man, coming into the world.<br><br>[* Or, *the true light which lighteth every man was coming.* † Or, *every man as he cometh.* |

### TIT. ii. 11.

| | |
|---|---|
| For the grace of God that bringeth salvation hath appeared to all men. | For the grace of God hath appeared,* bringing salvation to all men.<br><br>[* Or, *hath appeared to all men, bringing salvation.* |

With this amendment the Improved Version agrees. So also Dean Alford translates, but explains it to mean that God is willing that all men shall be saved (1 Tim. ii. 4), and has provided a salvation open to all. But the Revised Version reads there, 'who willeth that all men should be saved,' quite as strong an expression of Universalism as that above cited. So, in 1 Tim. iv. 10, where even the Old Version reads, 'We trust in the living God, who is the Saviour of all men,' the Revision certainly favours 'the larger hope' in the more genial strength and cogency of its expression, 'To this end we labour and strive, because we have our hope set on the living God, who is the Saviour of all men.'

# INDEX.

In this Index will be found reference to all the passages which are commented upon in the Work, not to such as are only alluded to.

The citations are made from the Revised Version, and M. means the margin of that Version; while the Authorized Version is indicated by the letters A.V.

**LUKE**

PAGE

v. 24. power to forgive sins [M. or, *authority* ............ 69

vi. 35. ye shall be sons of the Most High [A.V. the children of the Highest ...................................... 106

viii. 12. that they may not believe and be saved ............ 151

viii. 31. into the abyss [A.V. the deep ......................... 124

x. 15. thou shalt be brought down unto Hades [A.V. thrust down to hell.................................... 123

xii. 5. to cast into hell [M. Gr. *Gehenna* ................... 122

xii. 10. unto him that blasphemeth against the Holy Spirit [A.V. the Holy Ghost ............................ 46

xii. 12. the Holy Spirit shall teach you [A.V. the Holy Ghost shall teach you ............................ 49

xii. 46. his portion with the unfaithful [A.V. the unbelievers 15

xiv. 10. then shalt thou have glory [A.V. have worship ... 75

xvi. 23. in Hades he lifted up his eyes [A.V. in hell ...... 122

xviii. 30. and in the world to come eternal life [M. or, *age;* A.V. everlasting life ................................. 135

xx. 34, 35. the sons of this world marry . . . worthy to attain to that world [M. or, *age* .......................... 134

xx. 36. and are sons of God [A.V. the children of God... 106

xx. 47. receive greater condemnation [A.V. damnation... 126

xxii. 32. when once thou hast turned again [A.V. when thou art converted ...................................... 152

xxii. 69. from henceforth shall [A.V. hereafter shall........ 138

xxiii. 42. Jesus, remember me [A.V. Lord, remember me... 76

xxiii. 42. comest in thy kingdom [M. some read (as A.V.), *into thy kingdom*........................................ 76

xxiv. 52. they worshipped him [M. some omit this ......... 75


**JOHN**

i. 3, 10. all things were made . . . the world was made, by him [M. or, *through* ............ .................. 63

i. 9. there was the true light . . . coming [M. or (as A.V.), *which lighteth every man that cometh,* or, *as he cometh* ....................................... 159

i. 12. to them gave he the right to become children of God [A.V. power to become the sons ............ 155

i. 14. the only begotten from the Father [M. or, *an only begotten from a father*................................. 108

i. 15. he was before me [M. Gr. *first in regard of me* ... 98

N

Printed by C. Green & Son, 178, Strand.